P9-CNE-604

THE ORCHARD BOOKS

III : *Love Songs of Sion*

LOVE SONGS OF SION

A Selection of
Devotional Verse
from
Old English Sources
adapted by

NEVILE WATTS

LONDON
Burns Oates and Washbourne Ltd.
Publishers to the Holy See
1924

NIHIL OBSTAT:

G. H. JOYCE, S.J.,

Censor deputatus.

IMPRIMATUR:

EDM. CAN. SURMONT,

Vicarius generalis.

WESTMONASTERII,
  Die 2ᵃ Junii, 1924.

Made and Printed in Great Britain

MATRI

MATRI ECCLESIÆ

ET

MATRI SANCTORUM OMNIUM

G O, little treatise, require the folk of
grace
That shall of thee have inspection;
Be not too bold to appear in any place
Of malapertness nor presumption;
Thine author simple is, though of affection
He meaneth well; pray them that shall
thee read
With goodly support to do correction
Thee to reform, wheresoe'er they see need.

LYDGATE, *Trin. Coll. Camb. MS.*

INTRODUCTION

THE mainspring of a nation's life is its thought; and the quintessence of its thought is in its poetry. This statement, superficially true of poetry which is a conscious and deliberate reflection of contemporary feeling, as was that of Tennyson, is deeply true of that poetry which is the spontaneous and unfostered outgrowth of the spirit of an age. Such poetry is commonly anonymous, and naturally so; for the poet is merged in his society; he melts into the crowd to the sentiment of which he gives perfect utterance. Such was " Homer," such were our own ballad-writers, and such, save for the testimony of his compeers, might have been Shakespeare himself; and these were not single men, but epitomes each of his age. " I knew a very wise man," wrote Andrew Fletcher of Saltoun, " that believed that if a man were permitted to make all the ballads, he need not care who should make the laws of a nation." A wise man indeed; for the nameless makers of our ballads were, and are, makers of our history more than the legislators whose biographies we know; for while the former tell us what the people thought and loved, the record of our laws is but the record of what that people's rulers thought it better that they should not think and not love.

Furthermore, anonymity in poetry is not merely a title to its authenticity as the interpreter of a nation; it is also its own hall-mark of excellence. Anonymous poetry survives solely by its own virtue. Not buoyed up by the covers of any " Collected Works," it is *rerum immersabilis undis,* and no passing waves of popular disfavour can drown it. Much that is mere lumber and ballast floats upon the raft which is the name of Wordsworth; " Sumer is icumen in " breasts the billows proudly unsupported, hearing the surf that breaks upon the shore of eternity. Test this in any fitly-chosen anthology; is not the gleaning of " The Nut-Brown Maid," " Weep you no more, sad fountains," " Love will find out the way," " Phillida flouts me," and " O waly, waly, up the bank " more than all the vintage of many a great name ?

Nearly all the poems in this selection are anonymous. I do not claim for all of them outstanding excellence, though I venture to think that there is not one that merits oblivion; but I do claim that the poetry which they exemplify illuminates for us the *penetralia* of England's soul more searchingly than any other literary survival between Chaucer and Shakespeare. If I were to yield an exception, it would not be Surrey and Wyatt, who are of the Court, nor pre-Shakespearean drama, which is of the Schools, but the Miracles and the Moralities, which are of the people: and the exception would prove my rule. For when religious art is both popular and spontaneous, it is a proof that a popular and spontaneous religion lies at the heart of a nation's life. In both the seventeenth and the nineteenth centuries the output of religious verse was considerable, but in neither period was it either popular or spontaneous. In the former it was mystically and philosophically aloof; and in the latter it was, in all its successive waves, sectarian and indicative of tendencies that either did not persist or were not national—Evangelicalism, the Oxford Movement, Catholicism. Wesley, Keble, Francis Thompson, are great names, but they speak neither for nor from the heart of England.

But the poetry in this book is representative of no -isms, not even of Catholicism; it *is* representative of Catholic England, which is a very different thing. It is as native and as uncultured as the violet of the

xi

INTRODUCTION

English hedgerow; it sings in "native wood-notes wild" like the English thrush. We may push the similes further: like the violet, it is artless and unambitious; like the thrush, it is sometimes monotonous, singing "the selfsame passage o'er and o'er," not for the reason of Browning's "wise" bird, but because it never loses the "first, fine, careless rapture" that inspires it. That repetition must needs be vain repetition is a modern heresy, whose high priest is the American who begged to be shown everything in the Louvre, but to be shown nothing twice.

Of repetition there is in this poetry much, and of conventional phrase and epithet not a little, but it is the repetition of the rapture that can never say enough, and the verbal conventionality of the love that is too full to be solicitous of the *mot juste*. The rapture and the love at least are beyond gainsaying. The poems are mainly of the later fourteenth and the fifteenth centuries, and we are told that this age saw the dawn of disillusion in religion. But that the "illusion," among the rank and file of the people at least, was an unconscionable time in dying, let these poems bear witness.

Mark how certain "notes" of this poetry assert its integral unity with the continuous stream of English poetry. The leading trait of our minstrelsy throughout the ages has been its passionate love of Nature. But this is an under-statement. To the English folk-singer Nature is not a mistress, but an *alter ego*. Spring and autumn are no more in the year than in his own being. It is not that he takes his cue for mirth or mourning from the bursting of the bud or the fall of the leaf; it is rather that his soul and the seasons proceed in inseparable unison—a unison that is no " pathetic fallacy " but rather a poetic verity—the highest of all verities. When the unison is broken it is felt to be a cataclysmic shock, a lapse into chaos.

> How can ye chant, ye little birds,
> And I sae fu' o' care ?

This feeling of oneness with Nature is prominent in most of our early lyrics of earthly love. But the love lyric was in training for a higher love; and out of the erotic folk-minstrelsy grew a religious music that lost none of its fervour when it sloughed its carnality. Nay, it even gained the fervour of a greater directness; for it sped like an arrow to the heart of life, and no breeze of fancy deflected it. And here, too, Nature and the poet are at one. I give a stanza from a poem not included in this selection:

INTRODUCTION

When I see blossoms bursting,
    And hear blithe bird-notes sung,
With sweet love-longing thirsting,
    My raptured heart is stung.
All from a love that new is,
That joyous, full, and true is,
    My gladsome song hath sprung;
For sure I know that this is;
My joys, my hopes, my blisses,
    On him alone are hung.*

The reader will find a close counterpart of this in the wintry mood, if he will turn to No. 68 in this book; while No. 43 will give him an example of its converse, in which the singer cries out against the divorce between Nature and himself.

Thus this body of lyrical poetry attests the continuity of the Nature-tradition in our literature from Chaucer—whose absorption in humanity rarely allows his delicate feeling for Nature to appear—down to Shakespeare's glorious outburst at the end of *Love's Labour's Lost*. We deride ourselves as a nation for making the weather the staple of our conversation; but it is matter for pride rather than for shame, inasmuch as we show thereby that we have not lost that sensibility which has made our poetry unique in Europe. We have wrought

* Wright, *Specimens of Lyric Poetry*, No. 21; quoted in Ten Brink's *History of English Literature*, and modernised by the translator, H. M. Kennedy.

a music which is unsurpassed largely out of an intense self-identification with Nature and her passing moods.

I have spoken of the lyric of explicit passion, the passion which cannot say enough, and which expands and expends itself in repetitions and amplifications, turning its theme over and over and viewing it from this point and from that, in the manner of *Venus and Adonis* or Shelley's "Skylark" Ode. There is another and a rarer form, in which our language is rich, and which is the very attar of poetry. It is the lyric that verges on the inarticulate, because the singer is conscious of an absurd incongruity between his emotion and the means at his command for its expression. "Silence is the perfectest herald of joy," says Claudio in *Much Ado About Nothing;* "I were but little happy, if I could say how much." And there is an utterance which has all the effect of silence; whose words are no more symbols, but gestures; which says the least possible, because each syllable seems to chain to earth an emotion that paces among the stars. Of such are most of Sappho's fragments, Catullus' "Odi et amo," "Take, O take those lips away," "A slumber did my spirit seal," and "Break, break, break!" Of such, in this selection, are Nos. 20, 40, 45, 62, 72. The singer despairs of finding words to match the thought; he disdains to degrade its sanctity by effort foredoomed to defeat; so, after a placid phrase that is pregnant with eternity, he stands mute with bowed head. To the touch and to the eye it is frost; but to the understanding heart it is the perfervid incandescence that seethes about the sun.

Many of the poems in this selection are dramatic in their form, and a still larger number are dramatic in the concreteness of their conception. And, indeed, it was an age of objectivity that produced them, just as the age of Elizabeth which followed it was an age of objectivity passing towards the subjective. If Everyman and his companions typify the later Middle Age, Henry V may stand for the earlier part and Hamlet for the close of the Elizabethan Age. This is not to say, as is often asserted, that medievalism was materialistic. The objectivist pins his faith to an Absolute; but his Absolute is not of necessity material. Plato, the greatest objectivist of antiquity, was also the founder of Idealism; to him the Ideal was the only Real. The flaw in Plato's theory of life had been that, so far as we can perceive, he provided no link between the Ideal and the Real, between the world of being and that of becoming. But the

Middle Age, with that grasp of truth, completer than Plato's, which Christian revelation gave to it, knew of such a link in the doctrine of Transubstantiation. In repudiating this doctrine, the reformers, who thought that they were enthroning the Absolute in each individual bosom, banished it to an exile remoter than the remotest star. The traducers of the age blame it for its attachment to material forms of expression. The age did tend to express itself in the concrete; but this surely is neither surprising nor blameworthy in an age which believed that the Creator himself had done so.

Prominent among the manifestations of this concreteness of mind was the passion—for it was scarcely less—for dramatic representation. To the Middle Age, as Gaston Paris says, " the universe was a vast stage, on which was played an eternal drama, full of tears and joy, its actors divided between heaven, earth, and hell; a drama whose end is foreseen, whose changes of fortune are directed by the hand of God, yet whose every scene is rich and thrilling." The drama runs in the veins of the nation that produced Shakespeare, and though of late poetry has resigned its dramatic element to the novel, and though Browning alone, among nineteenth - century poets, saw humanity tri-dimensionally, still there are, perhaps, signs that the drama proper is about to reclaim its own. There is a strong dramatic element, as I have said, in many of these poems. Notice No. 15—a conversation between our Lady and a worshipper at the stable, with its chorus-like refrain; Nos. 36, 37, 44, 46, and 49 all are dramatic in their character.

I have thus, in a brief sketch, tried to point out how entirely this poetry is racy of the soil, and how it chimes true with the rich antiphon of English song throughout the centuries. I have drawn attention to some of its characteristics, but I have not enlarged upon its beauties; that would have been an impertinence, no less than it would have been impertinent to publish this selection, had I not believed that the poems possessed sufficient beauty to enable them to stand on their own merits.

As to whether what I have done in the way of adaptation will escape the charge of impertinence, I can only beg the reader to recognise how hazardous a task is that of one who would recast antique verse into a later mould. I am sufficiently warned by the example of Dryden's mutilation of Chaucer. I have touched nothing that I thought intelligible to a modern reader as it stood, though I fear that even so I may have brushed the bloom from more than one cluster of delicate grace and sweetness. Still, I had to choose between two evils: the one, of affronting the scholar and the expert; the other, of irritating the " general reader " —for whom the selection was primarily made—by presenting him with a series of linguistic enigmas. I have chosen to offend, if offend I must, the less numerous of these classes.

I have modernised the spelling, except in a few places in which I have retained a final sounded *e*, where the syllable was necessary for the metre. For the purposes of scansion, it should be borne in mind that the tendency at the time when these poems were written was to stress the final syllable. When rhyme has compelled me to retain an obsolete word, I have given its modern equivalent at the foot; but, apart from this, I have omitted all linguistic or critical apparatus as being alien to the purpose of the book. In past-tense verbs I have preferred to write simply " ed " rather than " d " or " èd," leaving it to the reader's sense of rhythm to decide whether syllabic value is to be preserved or not. I have included one post - Reformation piece (No. 74), as being essentially medieval in spirit.

Finally, it is a pleasure to me to thank the

INTRODUCTION

Editor of the Series for his constant help and encouragement, my wife for her invaluable aid as amanuensis, and Mr. Wilfrid Pippet for his delicate line drawings of the Symbols of the Passion.

NEVILE WATTS

STRATTON ON THE FOSSE,
February 11, 1924.

CONTENTS

*The dates given at the head of each poem are approxi-
mately those of the MSS. Many of the poems were,
of course, composed much earlier. In the case of
poems not anonymous, the approximate date of
composition is given.*

CONTENTS

PART THE THIRD

OF OUR BLESSED LORD'S PASSION

CONTENTS

PART THE FOURTH

OF OUR LADY

PART THE FIFTH

OF THE FOUR LAST THINGS

HYMN TO THE TRINITY
AND OUR LADY

1. HYMN TO THE TRINITY AND OUR LADY

Thornton MS. (c. 1450)

FATHER, Son, and Holy Ghost,
   Lord, to thee I make my moan,
   Steadfast King, whose might is most,
Awful God upon thy throne.
I pray thee, Lord, that thou thee haste
   To forgive what I have misdone.

Father of heaven, eternal day,
   I pray thee, Lord, that thou me lead
In stable truth of thy one way,
   At mine ending, that hour of dread.
Thy grace I ask both night and day,
   Have mercy now on my misdeed.
Of mine asking say me not nay,
   But help me, Lord, in all my need !

Sweet Jesu, that for me wast man,
   Hear thou my prayers both loud and still;
For all my sins since life began
   Full oft I sigh and weep my fill.
Full often have I been forsworn,
   When I have wrought against thy will;
O, let me never be forlorn,
   My Jesu, for my deeds of ill !

3

HYMN TO THE TRINITY

Holy Ghost, I pray to thee,
  Night and day with good intent,
In all my sorrows comfort me,
  Thy holy grace to me be sent;
And let me never bounden be
  In sin's eternal punishment,
By Mary's love, that maiden free,
  On whom thou didst of old descend.

I pray thee, Lady meek and mild,
  That thou pray for my misdeed,
For the love of thy dear Child,
  Whom thou sawst on Rood-tree bleed.
Ever and aye have I been wild,
  My sinful soul is ever in dread;
Mercy, Lady meek and mild,
  Help me ever in all my need.

Lord, as thou art full of might,
  Whose love is sweetest for to taste,
My life amend, my misdeeds right,
  For love of Mary, maiden chaste.
And bring me to that blissful sight,
  Thy joy to see, where joy is most,
To look on thee in heaven's height,
  Father, Son, and Holy Ghost!

PART THE FIRST
OF HOLY MASS AND COMMUNION

2. THE SACRIFICE OF THE MASS

Lydgate, Balliol MS. (*c.* 1430)

LOOK on this writing, man both old and
young !
Walk here beside me, if you can espy
Aught therein for your exhortation,
To make you to hear Mass more devoutly;
And somewhat to your helping you may
see,
That heareth Mass with true devout
intent,
Where God, in form of bread, his body
doth present.

The Church is called the spouse of Jesu
Christ;
The cause of his marriage is the holy
Mass,
Where daily at the altar offreth up the priest
The Son to the Father, that is no less.
Call, man, for thy petition, and look thou
not cease !
Let thy heart with great devotion
thereto relent,
Where God, in form of bread, his body
doth present.

7

The grievous oaths that thou forget
   In hearing of Mass are done away;
An angel also thy steps doth mete,
    And presenteth thee in heaven that same
      day,
     When thou at the church endeavour thee
      to pray,
      To worship that glorious and blessed
       Sacrament,
      Where God, in form of bread, his body
       doth present.

Thine age, at Mass, shall not increase;
   Nor sudden death that day shall not thee
     spill;
And without housel* if thou meet disease,
    It shall stand therefor; and believe thou
     this skill,
     That to hear Mass thou mayest have good
      will.
      These profitable benefits to thee be lent,
      Where God, in form of bread, his body
       doth present.

And if any of thy kin be departed hence,
   And suffer in purgatory abiding pain,
Thy prayer and thy Mass may deliver them
    thence,
   And of thy redemption make them fain.

* The last sacrament.

8

In heaven they shall do for thee the same,
  Before angels and saints ever splendent,
  Where God in glory his body doth
    present.

So of this Mass the meed is noble and great
  To livers on earth, but after death much
    more;
For when death from the body the soul doth
    fret,
    Then the number of thy Masses are anon
      upbore
    Into heaven among saints the Trinity
      before.
      Wherefore have joy that thine account
        is sent
      Where God in glory his body doth
        present.

Now I counsel thee, man, do after my rede,*
  When the priest goeth to Mass, if thou
    may, come,
And unless sickness let thee, bare thine head,
  And knock upon thy breast and say, *Cor
    mundum*
    Crea in me, Deus, et spiritum!
      Hear it forth to the end with meek
        intent,
      Where God, in form of bread, his body
        doth present.

* Advice.

3. AN EXHORTATION TO PRIESTS WHEN THEY SHALL SAY THEIR MASS

Lydgate (Trin. Coll. Camb. MS.)

YE holy priests, remember in your heart,
   When ye to holy Mass yourselves
      address,
With love and dread first meekly to advert
   The dignity of virtuous noblesse,
   The ghostly treasure, the heavenly great
      richesse,
Good incomparable, none can aright con-
   ceive,
   Quake ye for fear, and tremble with
      meekness,
The Lord of lords what time ye shall receive.

And next remember, on that other side,
   Against his goodness, your iniquity;
Weigh ye his meekness 'gainst your froward
      pride;
   Void ye all rancour, think on his charity;
   Weigh his patience against your cruelty;
Be shriven and contrite with humble in-
   tent;
   Say, "Jesu, mercy," kneeling on your
      knee,
Ere ye receive that holy Sacrament.

Be wisely ware, and take ye right good heed,
    Of all presumption and wilful hardiness;
Take not on you that office but with dread;
    With contrite heart your sinfulness repress;
    Let bitter tears wash all your wickedness,
With weeping eyes scour ye your conscience,
    And then receive with spiritual gladness
The Lord of lords of most magnificence.

Ye shall also most lovingly remember
    The sufferings of his painful passion,
How he was hurt and bled in every member,
    And suffered death for your redemption;
    Give thanks to him in humble affection,
Who for your sake was wounded in the side
    Beseech that Lord for mercy and pardon,
In perfect charity with you to abide.

Next, that ye have a ghostly appetite,
    By influence alone of Jesu's grace,
In him alone to set all your delight,
    With fervent love, your joy and your
        solace;
    In your heart make his dwelling-place
For your eternal consolation;
    Let him not out of your mind pass,
Repast of angels in the heavenly mansion

4. LYDGATE'S PRAYER AT THE HOLY COMMUNION

Lydgate (*Trin. Coll. Camb. MS.*)

HAIL, holy Jesu, our health, our ghostly
food,
Hail, blessed Saviour, here in form
of bread !
Hail, thou for mankind offered on the
Rood,
For our redemption with thy blood made
red,
Stung to the heart with a hard spear's
head;
Now, gracious Jesu, for thy woundes five,
Grant of thy mercy, ere that I be dead,
Clean shrift and housel, while I am here
alive.

O Lamb, up offered for man in sacrifice,
Nailed to the Cross of merciful meekness,
Whose blood down ran in very piteous
wise
To scour the rust of all my wickedness;
Of all my sins to thee I me confess;
Now, Lord, put not thy mercy in delay,
But grant me, Jesu, of thine high goodness,
Meek shrift and housel ere mine ending
day.

O blessed fruit borne of a pure Virgin !
  Who with thy passion boughtest me so
      dear,
For Mary's sake, thine eares down incline,
  Hear mine orison by mean of her prayer;
  Thee for to please teache me the manner,
Void of all virtue, save only of thy grace;
  Grant in the fashion that I see thee here
Thee to receive, while I have life and space.

My Lord, my Maker, my Saviour, and my
      King,
  When I was lost, thou wert my redemptor,
Support and succour here in this living,
  Against all enemies my sovereign pro-
      tector;
  My chief comfort in all worldly labour,
Grant me, Lord, confession, repentance,
  Ere I of death shall pass the sharpe shower,
Thee to receive unto thy pleasaunce.

Let thy Mother be present in this need,
  That I may claim, of mercy more than
      right,
Mine heritage, for which thou diddest bleed,
  And grant me, Jesu, of thy gracious might,
  Each day of thee for to have a sight,
For ghostly gladness till my life shall end,
  And in spirit to make mine hearte light,
Thee to receive, ere that I shall hence wend.

O Paschal Lamb, in Isaac figured,
  Our spiritual manna, bread contemplative,
Sent down from heaven, in which we be
      assured
    'Gainst all our foes, strongest comfortative,
    Tokened in Paradise upon the tree of life,
Which Adam should restore unto his place,
  Grant me, Jesu, for a restorative,
Thee to receive, ere that I hence shall pass.

As I said erst, of angels thou art food,
  Repast to pilgrims in their pilgrimage,
Celestial bread to children that be good,
    Figured in Isaac, thirty year of age,
    When thou to Calvary took thy passage,
O Jesu, mercy, grant ere I be dead,
  And ere decrepitus put me in dotage,
To have repast of thy celestial bread.

My ghostly trust, charity, hope, and faith,
  Mine advertence,* my mind and memory,
All this of sooth my soul unto thee saith;
    Have mercy on me, O sovereign king of
      glory,
    Who sittest high in the heavenly con-
      sistory;
Jesu, let mercy surmount thy rigour,
  That thy passion allay my purgatory,
First by receiving of thee, my Saviour.

* Reason.

5. THE VIRTUES OF THE MASS

Lydgate (Trin. Coll. Camb. MS.)

HEARING of Mass giveth a great
reward,
Ghostly health against all sickness,
And medicine, as teacheth Saint Bernard,
To people impotent, that plain for feeble-
ness,
To faint, refreshing in their weariness,
And unto folk that go on pilgrimage,
It maketh them strong, sets them in
secureness,
Graciously to complete their voyage.

The mighty man, it maketh him more
strong,
Recomforteth the sick in his languor,
Giveth patience to them that suffer wrong,
The labourer beareth up in his labour,
To thoughtful people refreshing and
succour,
Gracious counsel to folk disconsolate,
Sustaineth the feeble, conveyeth the
conqueror,
Maketh merchants their faires* fortunate.

* Business.

Maketh men more meek to their correction,
    In ghostly love fervent and amorous,
It giveth sweetness and delectation
    To all the people that be gracious;
    True obedience to folk religious,
Grace at departing, comforting in sorrow,
    Good speed, good hap, in city, town, and
      house,
To all that hear devoutly Mass at morrow.*

Thus is the Mass our spear and eke our
    shield,
    Our mighty helm, our sword, and our
      defence,
Our mighty castle, our shelter in the field,
    Our strongest bulwark 'gainst all violence;
    For who that ever abideth in reverence
Till *In Principio*, conclusion of the Mass,
    Grace shall guide him, and conduct his
      presence,
'Gainst all his foes of high estate or less.

All these things being weighed in balance,
    Let folk in morning early up arise,
First of intent to God to do pleasaunce,
    In their hearts wisely advertise;
    No time is lost during that service,
Wherefore let no man plainly be in doubt,
    But that God shall dispose in any wise
To increase all thing that they be gone about.

* Morning.

16

6. BONE PASTOR, PANIS VERE

Robert Grosseteste's " Castle of Love" (c. 1240)

GOD of all his marvels put us in good
mind,
     When he would in form of bread
dwell with mankind.
Through the virtue of Christ's words of the
     Sacrament,
That the priest rehearses at his Mass with
     good intent,
Bread into Christ's flesh and wine into his
     blood
Suddenly is turned, for man's ghostly
     food;
Neither bread nor wine is after sacring in
     the Mass,
But very God's flesh and blood, in their
     likeness.
There is of bread and wine savour, colour,
     and figure,
Lasting through God's will, against the
     course of nature:
But under this likeness is none other sub-
     stance
But God's body and his blood with their
     appurtenance.
This is God's deed, and passes man's wit:
He has mickle mead, that truly knows it.

If thou receive his flesh and blood worthily,
Thou shalt be as a quick limb of his body;
And if thou keep thee so out of deadly sin,
As a cousin of his thou shalt heaven win.
The Paschal Lamb in the old law that all
  men should eat,
And manna that God sent from heaven to
  his folk for meat,
And blood that was ever offered for cleansing
  of sin,
Were tokens of his Sacrament that our help
  is in.
If man will with all his might love this
  Sacrament,
And use it out of deadly sin, aye with good
  intent,
Neither tongue may well tell, nor heart may
  well think
The noble and ghostly profit of this meat
  and drink!

7. AN ORISON TO GOD'S BODY AT THE ELEVATION

Vernon MS. (XVth century)

WELCOME, Lord, in form of bread,
  In thine hands are quick and dead,
    Jesu is thy name !
Thou that art in Trinity,
Lord, have mercy upon me,
  And shield thou me from shame.

Hail, Jesu, God's own Son,
Holy Spirit from heaven come,
  King of all the earth !
Hail, Man, of most might,
Son of God, that art so bright,
  Of maiden was thy birth !

Hail, King ! Hail, Knight !
Hail, Man, of most might,
  Prince upon thy throne !
Hail, Duke ! Hail, Emperor !
Hail be thou, Governor,
  That all this world dost own !

Hail, flesh ! Hail, blood !
Hail, Man of mild mood !
  Hail be thou, King !
Hail, God, fairest !
Hail, Child best,
  That madest everything !

19

Hail, Fruit !   Hail, Flower !
Hail be thou, Saviour !
   For us thou wert dead:
Hail, God, full of might,
God's Son, that art so bright,
   In form thou art of bread !

8. MIRABILE MYSTERIUM

Balliol MS. (XVth century)

MAN is on earth for good and ill,
    And he must believe with all his will
    In that Sacrament of the altar,
That God himself made at his Supper.
          Mirabile !

Though it seem white, yet is it red;
It is flesh, but seemeth bread;
It is God in his manhead,
As he hung on a tree !
          Mirabile !

9. A PRAYER TO THE BLESSED SACRAMENT

Myrc's " Instruction for Parish Prie ts,"
Cotton MS. (c. 1450)

JESU, Lord, welcome thou be,
In form of bread as I see !
Jesu, by thy holy name,
Shield me to-day from sin and shame.
Shrift and housel grant me thou,
Ere that I shall hence go,
And true contrition for my sin,
That I may never die therein.
And, as thou wert of maiden born,
Suffer me not to be forlorn,
But when that I shall hence wend,
Grant me thy bliss without an end. Amen.

10. THE INVITATION

Harley MS. (end of XIVth century)

LORD, I cry by day and night,
　　Come to my Feast, that I have
　　dight.*

If it please my Lord the King to hear me pray,
Let him come to my Guesting, with us to
　game and play !

* Prepared.

11. FROM THE LAY-FOLK'S MASS-BOOK

Royal MS., Brit. Mus. (c. 1375)

(a) OF HOLY MASS

THE worthiest thing, of most goodness
In all this world, it is the Mass.
For if all clerks did nothing else,
But told the virtues of Mass-singing
And the profit of Mass-hearing,
They ne'er should compass the fifth part,
For all their wit and all their art,
Of all its virtues, meeds, and pardon,
To them that with devotion,
In cleanness and in good intent,
Do worship in this Sacrament.

(b) AT THE BEGINNING OF THE MASS

God, for thy goodness,
At the beginning of this Mass,
Grant to all that it shall hear
That they of sin be clean and clear.
Lord, save the priest that it shall say
From temptations to-day,
That he be clean in deed and thought,
That evil spirits vex him not;
That he fulfil this Sacrament
With stainless heart and good intent.

First, to do thee all honour,
That art sovereign of all succour;
And to thy Mother, maiden bright,
And to thy saints in heaven's light.
And give to all that hear soul-health,
Aid and grace and every wealth;
And to all those we have in mind,
Our friends and comrades, kith and kind,
Good Lord, grant them by this Mass
Of all their sins forgiveness.
And rest and peace that last alway
To Christian souls passed away;
And to us all thy succour send,
And bring us to joy without an end.   Amen.

(c) AT THE GOSPEL

Jesus, my love, grant me thy grace,
And for amendment might and space,
Thy word to keep and do thy will,
To choose the good and leave the ill;
And that it so may be,
Good Jesu, grant it me.   Amen.

(d) AT THE OFFERTORY

Jesus, born in Bethlehem town,
To thee the three sage kings came down,
And offered incense, gold and myrrh;
And thou didst watch them, far or near,
And thou didst guide them well all three
Home again to their countree;

So now our offerings that we offer,
And our prayers that we proffer
Take thou, Lord, to thy loving,
And be our help in every thing,
That all our perils may be past,
And grant good guerdon at the last;
And all our sins do thou amend,
And in our need us succour send.   Amen.

(e) At the Secret

Jesu, receive this our service
And this solemn sacrifice,
For thy priest and for us all
That now are here, or ever shall,
This Mass to hear or worship do,
The Host to see and pray thereto;
For all men living in God's name,
That they have help from sin and shame;
For all the souls that hence are past,
That they have rest that aye shall last.
    Pater Noster.   Ave Maria.   Credo.   Amen.

(f) At the Preface

In world of worlds without an ending
Thanked be thou, Jesu, my King.
All my heart I give to thee,
For right it is that so should be;
With all my heart I worship thee;
Jesu, blessed mayst thou be.

And with my heart I worship thee
For all the good thou dost to me.
Sweet Jesu, grant me now this,
That I may come unto thy bliss,
There with angels for to sing
This sweet song of thy loving,
Sanctus, Sanctus, Sanctus.
Jesu, grant that it be thus.   Amen.

(g) AT THE CANON

Lord, all honour be to thee.
With all my heart I worship thee.
I thank thee, Lord, as well I ought,
For all the good thou hast me brought,
That of thee I have received,
Since the time I was conceived.
My life, my limbs thou hast me lent,
And my right wit hast to me sent;
And thou hast kept me by thy grace
From perils sore in many a place.
All my life and all my living
Wholly have I of thy giving;
Dear thou bought'st me with thy blood,
And diedst for me upon the Rood.
I have done against thy will
Many times, both great and ill.
Thou art ready of thy goodness
For to grant me forgiveness,
And give me grace for to eschew
To do that thing that I should rue.

And let thy grace on us descend,
That so, at our long travail's end,
When we from all this world shall sever,
Joy may be ours that lasteth ever.   Amen.

(*h*) At the Elevation

Loved be thou, King,
And thanked be thou, King,
And blessed be thou, King,
     Jesu, my only joy,
For all the gifts thou givest me,
For the blood thou shed'st for me,
For the Cross thou bar'st for me;
Give thou me grace to sing
The song of thy loving.

Pater Noster.   Ave.   Credo.

(*j*) At the Memento of the Dead

Jesus, of thy holy grace,
Hear our prayers in this place.
Hear us, Saviour, when we pray
For Christian souls now passed away;
Let them by this Offering gain
Ease and respite of their pain.
Let our Mass be help indeed
Unto all in their most need,
Unto all we love so well,
That they 'scape the pains of hell.
Be it meed and medicine
To all in purgatory that pine.

Wipe the tears from out their eyes,
Loose their bonds and bid them rise
From their pain and woe at last
Into gladness never past.   Amen.

(k) At the Agnus Dei

Lamb of God, to thee we pray,
Do the sin of earth away;
Of thy mercy and thy ruth
Grant us peace our care to soothe.
Set our love on thee alone,
Come, and make our hearts thine own.
Fill us with thy perfect will
To choose the good and leave the ill.
Let my body and my soul
Serve thee as a perfect whole,
That both and each, of one assent
May serve thee with a good intent.
Jesu, Prince of Peace, we pray,
Peace be ours upon this day.
Let all striving be forgot
And all hate remembered not.
Let us now love each the other,
Even as brother loveth brother;
That by virtue of this Mass
We may have forgiveness
Of all our guilt and our misdeed,
And have thy bliss for our great meed.
Amen

(*l*) At the Post-Communion

Jesu, my King, in pity hear;
To my prayer bend down thine ear;
Stretch out thine everlasting arm
To shelter us from every harm.
And if death meet us by the way
All unawares upon this day,
We pray this Mass stand us instead
Of shrift and oil and housel-bread;
And, Jesu, by thy woundes five
Show us the way of righteous life.   Amen.

(*m*) A Thanksgiving before Leaving

God be thanked for all his works,
God be thanked by priests and clerks,
God be thanked by every man;
God be thanked for his goodness,
But most chiefly for this Mass.
May all prayers that here we pray
Unto God's throne find the way.
And by the holy sign I make
Let me God's own blessing take.
In Nomine Patris et Filii et Spiritus Sancti.
   Amen.

   Pater Noster.   Ave Maria.   Credo.

PART THE SECOND
OF OUR BLESSED LORD'S LOVE

12. (1) THE NAME OF JESUS

Lydgate's Testament (c. 1430)

WITHIN my closet and in my little
      couch,
    O blessed Jesu, and by my bedside,
So that no fiend or enemy shall me touch,
The name of Jesu shall with me abide.
My load-star is he and my sovereign good,
Throughout this world, whether by land or
    sea;
O Jesu, Jesu, for all folk provide,
Who to thy name devoutly bow the knee.

There is no love that perfectly is grounded,
But it of Jesu took its source supernal;
For upon him all perfectness is founded,
Our Tower, our Castle against foes infernal;
Our Portcullis, our Bulwark, and our Wall,
Our Shield, our Helm, 'gainst all adversity,
Our Heritage, and our Guerdon eternal,
To whom all living things shall bow the knee.

Do mercy, Jesu, ere that we hence pace
Out of this perilous, dreadful pilgrimage,
Beset with brigandage in every place,
With fell intent to hinder our passage:

33

I, above all, for I am fallen on age,
And sore enfeebled of old infirmity,
Cry unto Jesu for my sore outrage,
With all my heart thus kneeling on my knee.

Let not be lost that thou hast bought so dear,
Not with silver or gold, but with thy precious
    blood;
Our flesh is frail, and short our sojourn here,
The serpent old malicious is of mood.
The world unstable is, now ebb, now flood,
All things conclude in mutability,
'Gainst whose perils I hold this counsel good,
To pray for Jesu's mercy on our knee.

13. (2) A DEVOUT HUMBLE PRAYER

Lydgate's Testament (*c.* 1430)

O JESU, Jesu, hear mine orison,
 Bridle my lust beneath thy discipline,
 Quell sensuality, illume my reason
To tread the track of spiritual doctrine.
Let thy grace lead me straight as is a line,
With humble heart to live in thy pleasaunce
And, blessed Jesu, in my life's decline
Grant by thy grace shrift, housel, repentance.

Let me not rest, my soul have no quiet,
Occupy me with spiritual travail,
To sing and say, " O mercy, Jesu sweet."
My Guardian against fiends in my battail,
Let me put off all other apparel,
And in Jesu put all my confidence.
Treasure of treasures, that may most avail,
Grant, ere I die, shrift, housel, repentance.

Thou, Jesu, art my succour and refuge
'Gainst all the storms of tribulation,
That worldly billows with their fell deluge
O'erwhelm me not in their deep dungeon,
Where Charybdis hath domination,
And Circe singeth songs of disturbance:
To pass that danger be my protection;
Grant, ere I die, shrift, housel, repentance.

35

I feel my heart all frail and ruinous,
Unfit, O Lord, that thou therein shouldst
    rest;
But as a carpenter comes to a broken house,
Or an artificer repairs a riven chest,
So thou, Jesu, of craftsmen all the best,
Repair my thought broke with misgovern-
    ance;
Visit my soul, and through its steel walls
    burst;
Grant, ere I die, shrift, housel, repentance.

I cry to thee that diedst on the Rood,
Which with thy blood was stained and made
    red,
And on Sheer* Thursday gave us for our
    food
Thy blessed body, Jesu, in form of bread:
To me most sinful grant, ere I be dead,
To cleanse myself for mine inheritance.
O thou with sharp thorn crowned on thine
    head,
Grant, ere I die, shrift, housel, repentance.

* Maundy.

36

14. (3) THE LAMB OF SACRIFICE

Lydgate's Testament (c. 1430)

BEHOLD, O man, lift up thine eye and
see
What mortal pain I suffered for thy
trespass.
With piteous voice I cry and say to thee:
" Behold my wounds ! Behold my bloody
face !
Hear the rebukes that do me so menace,
Behold my foes that do me so despise,
And how that I, to bring thee back to grace,
Was like a lamb offered in sacrifice !

" Behold the heathen folk that did me take,
Behold the cords wherewithal I was bound,
Behold the spears that made mine heart to
quake,
Behold the garden wherein I was found.
Judas behold, his thirty pennies round,
Behold his treason and his covetise.
Behold how I, with many a mortal wound
Was like a lamb offered in sacrifice !

" Against thy pride behold my great meekness,
Against thine envy see my charity,
Against thy foulness see my chaste cleanness,
Against thy greed behold my poverty:

37

Between two robbers nailed to a tree,
Sprent with red blood, they would me so
 disguise,
Behold, O man, all this I did for thee,
Meek as a lamb offered in sacrifice !

" Behold my love, and give me thine again,
Behold, I died thy ransom for to pay;
See how mine heart is open, broad, and plain,
Thy ghostly enemies solely to affray;
An harder battle no man might assay,
Of triumphs all the greatest enterprise !
Wherefore, O man, no longer feel dismay,
I gave my blood for thee in sacrifice !

" Turn home again, thy sin do thou forsake:
Behold and see if aught be left behind,
How I to mercy am ready thee to take.
Give me thine heart, and be no more unkind.
Thy love and mine together do thou bind,
And let them never part in any wise.
When thou wert lost, thy soul again to find,
My blood I offered for thee in sacrifice !

" Tarry no longer; toward thine heritage
Haste on thy way, and be of right good cheer.
Go each day onward on thy pilgrimage:
And think how short is thine abiding here.
Thy place is built above the stars so clear,
No earthly home is built so stately-wise.
Come then, my friend; come, brother mine
 most dear,
For thee I gave my blood in sacrifice !"

15. THE COMING OF THE CHRIST-
CHILD

Balliol MS. (XVth century)

*M*ATER, *ora Filium,*
ut post hoc exilium
nobis donet gaudium
beatorum omnium !

Fair maiden, who is this Bairn,
That thou bearest on thine arm ?
Sir, it is a King's Son,
That in heaven above doth wone.*

Mater, ora, etc.

Man to father hath he none,
But himself is God alone;
Of a maid he would be born,
To save mankind that was forlorn.

Mater, ora, etc.

The kings brought him presents,
Gold and myrrh and frankincense,
To my Son, full of might,
King of kings and Lord of right.

Mater, ora, etc.

* Dwell.
39

Fair maiden, pray for us
Unto thy Son, sweet Jesus,
That he will grant us of his grace
In heaven high to have a place !

Mater, ora, etc.

16. RICHARD DE CASTRE'S PRAYER

Lambeth MS. (*c.* 1430)

JESU, Lord, that madest me,
    And with thy blessed blood hast
        bought,
Forgive that I have grieved thee
    In word, in will, and eke in thought.

Jesu, in whom is all my trust,
    Who died upon the awful Tree,
Withdraw my heart from fleshly lust,
    And from all worldly vanity.

Jesu, by the bitter smart
    In thy feet and thine hands two,
Make me meek and lowly of heart,
    And to love thee as I should do.

Jesu, by the bitter wound
    That pierced thee to thy heart's root,
From sin that hath my spirit bound
    Thy blessed blood must be my boot.*

And, Jesu Christ, to thee I call,
    For thou art God, and full of might,
Keep thou me clean, that I ne'er fall
    In deadly sin by day nor night.

* Aid.

41   C

Jesu, give me, when I pray,
  Patience to bear my strong disease,
That never may I do or say
  Aught that may thee, dear Lord, displease.

Jesu, by the deathly tears
  That thou sheddest for my guilt,
Hear and speed my feeble prayers,
  Let not my soul's blood be spilt.

Jesu, most comfortable sight
  To eyes that love thee everywhere,
Comfort all those in mournful plight,
  That bow beneath a load of care.

Jesu, keep them that have been good
  Amend all that have grieved thee,
And send them fruit of earthly food
  As each man needs in his degree.

Jesu, that art in very sooth
  Almighty God in Trinity,
Make wars to cease, and send us peace,
  With lasting love and charity.

Jesu, thou spiritual Rock
  Of Holy Church, that is of old,
Make of all men one single flock,
  Beneath one Shepherd, in one Fold.

And Jesu, by thy blessed blood,
  Bring, if thou wilt, the souls to bliss
Of all those that have done me good,
  And let them never do amiss! Amen.

17. A PRAYER FOR MERCY
Thornton MS. (*c.* 1440)

1.

JESU, that died on the Rood for love of me,
　And bought me with thy precious blood,
　　have mercy on me.
What thing soe'er it be that lets me from
　loving thee,
Be it my love, be it my hate, do it away from
　me.

2.

Jesu, of whom all true love springs,
That for my love hath suffered pain,
To lusty love of earthly things
Suffer me never turn again.
In thy love be my liking,
And thereto make me glad and fain,
And for thy love to make mourning,
That for my love would be slain.
Amen.　Amen.　Amen for charity.

Shield us from the pains of hell,
That bitter are to bear and fell,
And with thy grace fulfil us all,
That ready we may be to thy call;
And let us never part from thee,
As thou for us died on a tree.
Grant us, Lord, that it so be.
Amen.　Amen.　Amen for charity.

43

18. A PRAYER TO JESUS

Thornton MS. (c. 1440)

JESU CHRIST, have mercy on me,
As thou art King of majesty.

And forgive me my sins all,
That I have done, both great and small.

And bring me, if it be thy will,
To dwell in heaven with thee still! Amen

19. THE STRANGER

Harley MS. (end of XIVth century)

"WHO art thou that comest, so meek,
yet in such splendour?
Who art thou that comest, a Child,
yet so all-wise?
Who art thou that comest, so dreadful, yet
so tender?
Who art thou that comest, so poor, yet so
almighty?"

" I am a Knight, for you to fight;
I am a Pleader, to win you right;
I am a Master, to lesson you;
I am a King, and a Comrade true!"

44

20. GOD'S GOODNESS

Harley MS. (end of XIVth century)

HE abideth patiently;
He forgiveth easily;
He understandeth mercifully;
And he forgetteth utterly.

21. MERCY

Harley MS. (end of XIVth century)

IF sin were not, then mercy were not;
When mercy is called, she cometh
anon.

Mercy is readiest where sin is most;
Mercy is latest where sin is least.

Mercy abideth and waiteth all day,
Till man from sin will turn away !

22. THE COMPLAINT OF CHRIST

Lambeth MS. (c. 1465)

THIS is the complaint of God
　　To every man that he hath bought,
　And thus he saith in bitter plaint:
" Mine own people, what have ye wrought
That ye to me are so faint,
　And I your love so sore have sought ?

" Let your answer be unfeigned,
　For I know your every thought.
Have I not done all I ought ?
　Have I left anything behind ?
Why are ye cold ?　I grieve ye not:
　Why are ye to your Friend unkind ?

" I shewed ye love; and that was seen,
　When I made ye like to me.
All creeping things and grasses green,
　I made them subject unto ye.
And from Pharaoh, that was so keen,
　Of Egypt, I delivered ye.

" And him and his slew unforeseen.
　The Red Sea sunderwise to flee
I bade that it should dry land be;
　I ceased the water and the wind;
I led ye o'er and made ye free;
　Why are ye to your Friend unkind ?"

23. SERVE AND LOVE CHRIST
Thornton MS. (*c.* 1440)

ON Christ cast thou thy thought,
　　Hate all thy wrath and pride;
　And think how he hath bought
Thee with wounds deep and wide.
When thou his love hast sought,
　　Then all shall well betide;
Of riches reck thou nought,
　　That from hell he may thee hide.

They turn their day to night,
　　That love their earthly sin,
And fail in that fell fight,
　　Wherein our souls we win.
For since they love unright,
　　And cannot cease therein,
They lose the land of light,
　　And are all dark within.

In Christ find thy solace,
　　Let his love change thy cheer;
With joy take thou his grace,
　　And hold him ever near.
That, seeking still his face,
　　Thy soul from sin be clear.
High he ordains thy place,
　　If thou his word wilt hear.

Then love him while thou may,
  The King of majesty;
Thy grief shall fly away,
  Thy joy return to thee.
Thy night shall turn to day,
  Thy bliss shall steadfast be.
When thou art as I say,
  I pray thee think on me.

Lord, wound with love within,
  And lead me to thy light:
Make thou me clean of sin,
  That nought may me affright.
As thou, to save thy kin,
  Didst dare death's awful might,
Grant me thy grace to win
  The guerdon of thy sight.

Then raise thine heart on high,
  And quell the bitter fiend,
And let thy soul still sigh
  To meet the blissful end.
And when thy death draws nigh,
  And thou shalt heavenward wend,
Thou'lt see him with thine eye,
  And come to Christ, thy Friend!

24. A SONG IN PRAISE OF LOVE

Lambeth MS. (c. 1430)

LOVE is life that lasteth aye,
　　As in Christ appeareth well;
　Weal nor woe can make away
　Love, as wisest sages tell.
Night it turneth into day,
　Turneth travail into rest;
If thou wilt do as I thee say,
　Thou shalt then be with the best.

Love is a thought of great desire,
　And also of a fair loving;
Love I liken to a fire,
　That may slacken for no thing.
Love us cleanseth of our sin,
　Love to us our bliss shall bring,
Love the hearts of kings may win,
　Love of every joy may sing.

The help of love is lifted high,
　For unto lofty heaven it ran;
Methinks in heart that it is sly,
　For it maketh folk both pale and wan.
Yet all is bliss when love draws nigh
　(I tell you it is as I can).
To win this love we needs must sigh,
　For ever it coupleth God with man.

Learn to love if thou wilt live
  When thou shalt hence fare;
All thy thought to him thou give,
  That he may keep thee from care.
Let not thy will from him depart
  Though thou wander the world o'er:
So thou may hold him in thy heart,
  And love him truly evermore.

The joy that on the earth is seen
  Is like unto the flowers gay;
Now they bloom, fair, fresh, and green,
  Now anon they fade away.
Such is the world, and aye has been,
  And will be aye until Doomsday,
Full great travail and much teen,*
  And escape them no man may.

Do but leave evil in thy thought,
  And hate the filth of sin,
And give to him that dear thee bought
  To rule thy heart within;
All thy soul thy Lord hath sought,
  Let him thy soul then win:
Thus shalt thou to bliss be brought,
  And shalt dwell aye therein.

In sooth the way of love is this:
  Trusty it is and true,
It standeth ever in stableness,
  And changeth ne'er for a new.

* Trouble.

50

The man who once that love may find,
  Or who in heart it knew,
From care it turns away his mind:
  Such mirth is found by few.

Learn, then, as I thee bid, this love:
  True love is Christ, as I thee tell.
With angels take thy place above:
  Buy joy, and never sell.
Love thou no love that withereth,
  But look that thy love may dwell;
For love is stronger far than death,
  And lasteth more than hell.

Love is light and a burden fine,
  Love gladdeth both young and old;
Love is without sorrow or pine,
  As lovers have me told.
Love to the soul is sweet as wine,
  It maketh both glad and bold;
To that love I shall so fast twine,
  That aye I may it hold.

Love is the fairest, sweetest thing
  Of all things earthly known;
Love is God's own darling,
  Love bindeth blood and bone.
In love therefore be our liking;
  Know we but love alone;
For truly by true loving
  Love maketh two but one.

But all fleshly love shall fare
   As do the flowers of May,
And shall be lasting no more,
   But as it were an hour of a day;
And sorrow cometh anon full sore,
   Her lust, her pride, and all her play;
And they are cast in bitter care,
   And pain that lasteth aye.

When their bodies in the fen lie,
   Then shall their souls be dread,
For up again they needs must hie,
   And answer for all their misdeed;
And if they then be seen in sin,
   And earthly life on earth have led,
Then shall they lie hell within,
   And have deep gloom for mead.

The rich men then their hands shall wring,
   That they wrought so evilly,
In flames of fire that smart and sting,
   With care and sorrow shamefastly.
If thou wilt love, then shalt thou sing
   To thy Lord Christ in melody,
For his love o'ercomes everything;
   In that love live we and die.

Jesu, God's only Son thou art,
   Lord of high majesty,
Send thy true love into mine heart,
   Only to covet thee.

Rive me of liking of this world,
   That thou my love may be;
Take mine heart into thy ward,
   Set me in stablety.

Jesu, thou, the maiden's Son,
   That with thy blood me bought,
Pierce my soul with thy spear anon,
   That in men love hath wrought.
Ah, wouldst thou bring me to thy sight,
   And fix on thee my thought,
In thy sweetness make mine heart light,
   That woe may wax to nought.

Jesu, my God and lovely King,
   Forsake not my desire.
Mine heart so high do thou low bring,
   I hate both pride and ire.
Thy love is all my desiring,
   Kindle thou, then, love's fire,
That I by thy sweet loving
   With angels may take my hire.

Jesu, put into my soul
   The memory of thy pine,
That both in joy and dole
   Thy love be ever mine;
My joy is all of thee,
   My soul take thou as thine;
May my love waxing be,
   And ne'er from thee decline.

My love is ever in sighing,
    While I dwell in this way;
My love is ever in longing,
    That bindeth me night and day,
Till I come unto my King,
    Where I dwell with him may,
And see his fair shining,
    In life that lasteth aye.

25. A DEVOUT THANKSGIVING

Lincoln Cath. MS. (XVth century)

ALMIGHTY God in Trinity,
  Inwardly I thank thee
  For thy good deed that thou me
wrought,
And with thy precious blood me bought,
And of all good thou givest me,
  Lord, blessed mayst thou be !
Honour, joy, and loving
Be to thy name without ending !   Amen.

26. THE CONSTANT LOVER

Chaucer (end of XIVth century)

O YOUNGE freshe folkes, he or she,
    In which that love up-groweth with
        your age,
Repair ye home from worldly vanity,
And of your heart up-cast ye the visage
To that one God that after his image
You made, and think ye all is but a fair,
This world, that passeth soon as flowers fair.

And love ye him, who did for his true love
Upon a Cross, our soules for to buy
First die, and rose, and sat in heaven above;
For he is false to no man, dare I say,
That will his heart all wholly on him lay.
And since he best to love is, and most meek,
What needeth feigned loves for to seek?

27. THE KING'S ADVICE TO HIS SON

Harley MS. (end of XIVth century)

SIN and filth do thou forsake,
   Cleanness of life for my love take.

Love God both with heart and thought,
For to his likeness thou art wrought.

Without love thou art forlorn:
Who hath not love were best unborn.

Of all thy weal I ask no more
But love me well for evermore.

Come, my sweet child, whene'er thou wilt,
For ready is thine heritage, forgiven thy guilt!

28. QUIA AMORE LANGUEO

OR, CHRIST'S COMPLAINT FOR HIS SISTER,
MAN'S SOUL

Lambeth MS. (c. 1430)

IN the valley of Restless Mind
  I sought, on mountain and on mead,
  Trusting a true love for to find:
Upon a hill then I took heed,
A voice I heard that did me plead,
In huge dolour complaining so:
  " See, dear soul, how my sides bleed,
    Quia amore langueo."

Upon this hill I found a tree,
  Under this tree a man sitting;
From head to foot wounded was he,
  His heart's blood I saw bleeding;
  A seemly man to be a King,
A gracious face to look unto.
  I asked him how he had paining,
    He said: " *Quia amore langueo.*

" I am true love that false was never,
  My sister, man's soul, I loved her thus:
Because I would in no wise dissever,
  I left my kingdom glorious;
  I prepared her a palace precious,
She fleeth, I follow, I loved her so:
  I suffered this paining piteous,
    Quia amore langueo.

" My fair spouse and my love so bright,
   I saved her from beating, and she hath me
      beat;
I clothed her in grace and heavenly light,
   This bloody shirt she hath on me set.
   From longing of love I will not let,
Meekly I bide her strokes: for lo,
   I have loved her ever, as I her said,
     Quia amore langueo.

" I crowned her with bliss, and she me with
     thorn;
   I led her to life, and she me to die;
I brought her to worship, and she me to
     scorn;
   I did her reverence, and she me villainy.
   My love to win hers hath no mastery;
Yet her hate made never my love her foe:
   I love her: ask me no question why,
     Quia amore langueo.

" Look thou upon my hands, O man.
   These gloves she gave me when I her
     sought.
They be not white, but red and wan,
   Embroidered with blood my spouse them
     brought.
   They will not off, I loose them not,
I woo her with them where'er she go;
   These hands for her so friendly fought,
     Quia amore langueo.

" Marvel not, man, that I sit still.
 See, love hath shod me wondrous strait;
She buckled my feet, as was her will,
 With sharp nails: ' Lo, thou mayest wait.'
 In my love was never deceit,
Her all my members I opened unto;
 My body I made her heart's bait,
  Quia amore langueo.

" In my side have I made her a nest,
 Look in ! how wide a wound is here !
This is her chamber: here shall she rest,
 That she and I may sleep secure.
 Here may she wash, if any filth were;
Here is refuge for all her woe,
 Come when she will, she shall have cheer,
  Quia amore langueo.

" I will abide till she be ready,
 I will her sue, if she say me nay;
If she reck not, I will be greedy;
 If she despise me, I will her pray.
 But if she weep that afar I stay,
My arms are wide-spread her to woo.
 Do but cry: ' I come.' Let thy soul assay,
  Quia amore langueo.

" I sit on this hill for to see far,
 I look to the valley my spouse to see;
Now runs she wayward, now comes she near,
 But out of my sight she may not flee.

There are foes in ambush to make her their
    prey,
But I run before her to banish her foe:
    Return, my spouse, again to me,
        Quia amore langueo.

" My fair sweet love, let us go play.
    Apples be ripe in my garden;
I shall thee clothe in new array,
    Thy meat shall be milk and honey and wine,
    Now, dear soul, let us go dine,
Thy sustenance in my scrip is, lo !
    Tarry thou not then, fair spouse mine,
        Quia amore langueo.

" If thou be foul, I shall make thee white;
    If thou be sick, I shall thee heal;
For thy mourning thou shalt have delight;
    Why wilt thou not, love, with me deal ?
    Foundest thou ever a love so leal ?
What wouldest thou, spouse, that I should do?
    Lo, in my mercy I thee appeal,
        Quia amore langueo.

" What shall I do with my fair spouse,
    But abide her, of my gentleness ?
Till that she look out of her house
    Of fleshly affection ?   My love she is.
    Her bed is made; her pillow is bliss;
Her chamber is ready, high and low;
    Look out on me at the window of kindness,
        Quia amore langueo.

" My love's in her chamber. Hold your
     peace;
  Make ye no noise, but let her sleep;
My babe shall be vext with no dis-ease,
  I would not hear my dear child weep.
  Within my breast I shall her keep,
Wonder not that I tend her so:
  This hole in my side had been ne'er so deep,
    But *Quia amore langueo.*

" Long and love thou never so high,
  My love is more than thine may be;
Weep thou, or joy thou, I sit thee by;
  Ah, wouldst thou but once, love, look on
    me !
  Spouse, must I always feed thee
With children's meat ?   Nay, love, not so.
  I will prove thy love with adversity,
    Quia amore langueo.

" Wax not weary, mine own dear wife;
  What meed is it to live ever in comfort ?
In tribulation I reign more rife
  Oftentimes than in disport.
  In weal and in woe I am there to support;
Then, dear soul, never from me go;
  Thy merit is most when thou art hurt,
    Quia amore langueo."

29. WHY ART THOU FROWARD
SINCE I AM MERCIABLE?

*Lydgate, Cam. Univ. Lib. MS. (early XVth
century)*

UPON a cross nailed I was for thee,
    And suffered death to pay thy dear
       ransom.
Forsake thy sin: I gave my life for thee:
Repent, and make sincere confession.
To contrite hearts I give remission.
Despair not then; I am not vengeable.
'Gainst ghostly foes think on my Passion:
    Why art thou froward since I am merci-
      able?

My bloody wounds that dripped upon the
    Tree
Look on them well and have compassion;
The crown of thorns, the spear, and the
    nails three,
Pierced hand and foot by indignation,
My heart riven for thy redemption:
Let us twain in this thing be agreeable,
Loss for loss, by just convention:
    Why art thou froward since I am merci-
      able?

Think in thy pride on my humility;
School well thine heart, and mind well this
    lesson:
Art envious ?   Think then on my charity,
My blood that trickled for thee drop by drop;
All this I did to save thee from prison;
Before thine heart, then, let this image dwell,
Sweeter than balm to sain* all ghostly poison:
    Why art thou froward since I am merciable?

* Heal.

30. THE LOVE OF JESUS

Lambeth MS. (c. 1430)

I SIT and sing of love-longing,
   That in my breast is bred;
Jesu, my joy, my heavenly King,
Why am I not thee-ward led?
Ah, surely then in all my yearning,
   And all my joy, I should be fed.
Jesu, bring me unto thy dwelling,
   By the blood that thou hast shed!

Doomed was he on a Cross to hang,
   He, the fair angels' food,
And his back sore scourges stang,
   As in his bonds he stood.
His breast was blue with beating,
   Not wasted was his blood,
And the thorn crowned that King,
   That was slain on the Rood!

White was his breast and bare,
   And red his bloody side,
Wan was his face so fair,
   His wounds were deep and wide.
Blanched was his bright eye,
   His flesh with bloody weals wet.
Who would not stand and sigh,
   To see that lovely life forth-let?

Death and life began to strive
    Which should be master there:
Dead life rose again to life,
    That to bliss we might fare.
I sigh and sob both day and night
    For him that is so fair of hue,
And nought shall make my spirit light,
    Save his love that is so true.

Whoso hath Jesu in his sight,
    And tasteth how sweet he is,
His mourning shall turn to blitheness
    bright,
    His longing into bliss.
In mirth he liveth night and day,
    That loveth that sweet Child;
Wrath from him shall all away,
    Were he never so wild.

And none of all mankind can tell
    The sweetness of his love:
Who in that love shall steadfast dwell
    His joy lasts aye above.
God shield we ne'er go down to hell,
    Who in love-longing grow not old,
Or that his foes him ever quell,
    Or that his love should e'er be cold.

Jesu is love that lasteth aye,
    In him is all our longing;
'Tis he that turneth night to day,
    And darkness into dayspring,

Jesu, think on me, I pray,
   For thee I hold my King;
And give me grace that so I may
   Love thee without an ending !   Amen.

31. A DEVOUT HYMN TO JESUS

Lambeth MS. (c. 1430)

JESU, who can thy sweetness see,
 And learn thereof the wondrous truth,
  To him all earthly love shall be
Bitter, save thine, in very sooth.
I pray thee, Lord, teach thou me clear
 In thy dear love to find my bliss,
And fix my heart alone on thee,
 For O, thy love what joy it is !

He is to me as mother dear,
 For ere my birth he did me heed,
And then in Baptism washed me clear,
 All smirched with sin by Adam's deed
With mighty meat he nurtured me,
 For with his flesh he would me feed;
A better food may no man see,
 To lasting life it will us lead.

He is my Brother and Sister too,
 For once he said and taught right clear,
That who his Father's will should do,
 Sisters and brothers to him were,
And as he did his kin us call,
 Full truly do I trust, therefore,
That he will never let me fall,
 But with his mercy heal my sore.

After his love needs must I long,
    For he my love full dear hath bought,
And when I went from him in wrong,
    From heaven to earth then he me
        sought.
For me he did his glory change,
    And all his noblesse set at nought,
He suffered need and penance strange,
    To bliss again ere he me brought.

His sides all blue and bloody were,
    That sometime were so white of
        hue,
His heart was pierced with a spear,
    His bloody wounds none but would
        rue.
My ransom sure he offered there,
    And gave his life for guilt of me.
His doleful deed doth cost me dear,
    And pierce my heart for pure pity.

To heaven then rose he with much
    bliss,
    When he had won his sore battail;
His banner broad displayed is,
    Whene'er my foe would me assail.
Well ought my heart then to be his,
    For he's the Friend will never fail,
And all that he desireth is
    But true love for his hard travail.

Lord, by the sweets that in thee bide,
    Have me in mind when I shall wend;
With steadfast truth my spirit guide,
    And defend me from the fiend.
Forgive me all I do amiss,
    Lest through my sins I enter hell,
But bring me, Lord, unto thy bliss,
    For evermore with thee to dwell !

32. BE MY COMFORT, CHRIST JESUS

Lambeth MS. (*c.* 1400)

JESU, that sprang of Jesse's root,
    As prophets old to us impart,
  So soft and mild in flower and fruit,
  So sweet in savour to man's heart,
Help, Jesu, unto me thou brought,
  When Gabriel first did Mary greet,
To fell our foemen under foot.
  In her thou sawst a seemly seat.
A maiden was thy mother meet,
  Of whom thou tookest flesh for us:
Lord, salve my sorrow, I entreat,
  And be my comfort, Christ Jesus!

Jesu, wisest of all wit,
  From thy Father full of might,
Man's soul that thou might succour it,
  In poor apparel thou wert dight;
Jesu, thou wert in cradle knit,
  And in weeds wrapt both day and
      night,
In Bethlehem born, as Gospel writ,
  With angels' song and heaven's light .
Born Babe unto a damsel bright;
  Full courteous was thy comely kiss.
By virtue, then, of that sweet sight,
  So be my comfort, Christ Jesus!

71

Jesu, that wert of years so young,
    Fair and fresh of flesh and hue,
When thou wert in thraldom hung,
    And tortured by full many a Jew:
When blood and water were outwrung,
    For beating was thy body blue:
As a clod of clay thou wert forth-flung,
    And men thy lifeless limbs out-threw.
But grace from out thy tomb grew:
    Alive, thou rose to comfort us.
For love of her that thy mind knew,
    So be my comfort, Christ Jesus!

Jesu, true God and very man,
    Two kinds knit in one person,
The wonder-work that thou began
    Thou hast fulfilled in flesh and bone:
Out of this world thou straightway wan,
    And lifted up thyself alone;
For mightily thou rose, and ran
    Straight to thy Father on the throne.
Now dare man no more make moan,
    For 'twas for man thou diddest thus,
And God with man is made at one,
    So be my comfort, Christ Jesus!

Jesu, our pure and loving Friend,
    Blest was the maiden that bare thee,
When thou for her at length did send,
    In heaven's bliss with thee to be;
When she from out this world did wend,
    Body and soul had majesty

Higher than any of angels' kind.
   On throne before the Trinity,
There may the Son his mother see
   In heaven on high to cherish us.
Thou peerless princess, pray for me,
   And be my comfort, Christ Jesus !

Jesu, my Sovereign Saviour,
   For whither else shall poor men go ?
Lord Christ, be thou my Governor,
   Let me not lose the faith I know.
Jesu, my joy and my succour,
   For body and for soul also
Best food be thou for evermore,
   And guide thou me through all my woe.
Thou mak'st him friend who erst was foe;
   Let me not live in languor thus,
But in my sorrow gladness shew,
   And be my comfort, Christ Jesus !

Jesu, to thee I cry and plead:
   Great Prince of Peace, to thee I pray;
For thou didst bleed for mankind's need,
   And suffer many a fearful fray.
Do thou me feed in all my dread
   With steadfast patience now and aye,
My life to lead in word and deed
   As most shall please thee thine own way.
Grant me good death when falls my day.
   Jesu, that died on Tree for us,
Let me not be the fell fiend's prey,
   But be my comfort, Christ Jesus !

33. A SONG OF LOVE-LONGING
Bodleian MS. (XVth century)

I

SWEET Jesu, now will I sing
   To thee a song of love-longing;
   Make in my heart a well to spring,
To love thee above everything.

Sweetest Jesu, mine heart's light,
Thou art day without the night;
Give me now both grace and might
For to love thee aright.

Sweetest Jesu, mine heart's gleam,
Brighter than the sun's beam,
As thou wert born in Bethlehem,
Make thou in me thy love-dream.

Sweet Jesu, my soul's food,
Every work of thine is good;
Thou boughtest me upon the Rood,
And sheddest thereon thy sweet blood.

Sweetest Jesu, Bairn best,
Thy love within mine heart make fast;
When I go north, south, east, or west,
In thee alone find I my rest.

Sweet Jesu, happy shall he be,
That thee in all thy bliss shall see.
With cords of love, then, draw thou me,
That I may come and dwell with thee.

Sweet Jesu, heaven's King,
Fairest and best of everything,
Bring me into that love-longing,
To come to thee at mine ending.

II

Jesu, sweet is the love of thee;
Nothing else may so sweet be;
Nought that man may think or see
Hath any sweetness against thee.

Jesu, no song may be sweeter,
Nor in the heart thought blissfuller,
Nor any feeling lightsomer,
Than thou, so sweet a Lover.

Jesu, thy love was given so free,
That it from heaven's height brought thee;
For love full dearly boughtest thou me,
For love thou hungst on the Rood-tree.

Jesu, to thy disciples dear
Thou saidest with full dreary cheer,
As they sat together there,
A little ere thou taken were,

Jesu, thou saidest that thou were
Full of sorrow and heart-sore,
And bade them tarry awhile there,
While thou besoughtst thy Father's ear.

To him thou saidst, " If it may be,
Dear Father, I pray to thee,
That this pain pass away from me:
As thou wilt so let it be."

Jesu, when thou to pray began,
The sweat of blood from thee ran:
From heaven an angel lit then,
And comforted thee, God and man.

(Mary, mild and innocent,
Pray for me—thou art present—
When my soul is from me went,
That it may have good judgement.)

Jesu, for love thou suffredst wrong,
Wounds sore and pains strong;
Thy pains so rueful were and long,
I may not tell them in my song.

Sweet Jesu, thou didst hang on Tree,
Not for thy guilt, but all for me;
For sins and guilt done against thee,
Sweet Jesu, forgive them me.

Jesu, when thou tormented were,
Thy pains waxed ever more and more;
Thy mother still with thee was there,
With sighings sorrowful and sore.

Jesu, how sawest thou in me
Aught that was needful unto thee,
That thou so hardly on the Tree
For me wouldest pained be?

Jesu, why wert thou so jealous,
Why so fervent and so zealous,
To buy at price so precious
Wretched man so vicious?

Jesu, my Leman, thou art so free,
All thou didst was for love of me;
What shall I for that yield thee?
Thou askest nought save love of me.

Jesu, my God, my Lord, my King,
Thou askest me none other thing,
But true love and heart-longing,
And love-tears and still mourning.

Sweet Jesu, needs must I love thee,
For thou hast shewn me thy Rood-tree,
Thy crown of thorns and thy nails three,
And the sharp spear that pierced thee.

Therein I see love's tokening:
Thine arms spread wide for love-embracing,
Thine head bowed for love-kissing,
Thy side all open for love-shewing.

Jesu, when I think on thee,
And look upon the Rood-tree,
And thy sweet limbs all bleeding see,
Lord, make that sight to wound me.

77

Jesu, thy mother that by thee stood,
Of love-tears she wept a flood;
'Twas thy wounds and thine holy blood
That made her have so drear a mood.

(Mary, I pray thee, as thou art free,
Of thy sorrow share with me,
That I may sorrow here with thee,
And partner of thy bliss be.)

Jesu, make me do thy will,
Now and ever, loud and still;
With thy love my soul fulfil,
And suffer never that I do ill.

Jesu, thy love is sweet and strong,
My life doth all thereto belong;
Teach me, Lord, thy love-song,
With sweet tears ever among.

Jesu, that dearly boughtest me,
Make me worthy to come to thee;
All my sins forgive thou me,
That I may come and dwell with thee.

Jesu all fair, my Leman bright,
I thee beseech with all my might,
Bring my soul into thy light,
Where is day and never night.

Jesu, thy bliss hath no ending,
There is no sorrow nor weeping;
But peace and joy with great liking;
Sweet Jesu, thereto us bring.   Amen

PART THE THIRD
OF OUR BLESSED LORD'S PASSION

34. THE FALCON

Richard Hill's Commonplace Book, Balliol MS. (c. 1520)

HE bare him up, he bare him down,
He bare him into an orchard brown.
    Lully, lulley, lully, lulley!
    The falcon hath borne my Mate away.

In that orchard there was an hall,
That was hanged with purple pall.
        Lully, lulley, *etc.*

And in that hall there was a bed,
That was hanged with gold so red.
        Lully, lulley, *etc.*

And in that bed there lieth a Knight,
His wounds bleeding day and night.
        Lully, lulley, *etc.*

By that bed's side there kneeleth a May,*
And she weepeth both night and day.
        Lully, lulley, *etc.*

And by that bed's side there standeth a stone,
" Corpus Christi " written thereon.
    Lully, lulley, lully, lulley!
    The falcon hath borne my Mate away.

* Maiden.

35. A DEVOTION ON THE SYMBOLS OF THE PASSION

Bodleian MS. (XVth century)

THE VERNACLE

O VERNACLE, I honour him and
    thee,
That thee made through his
    privity;
The cloth he set upon his face,
The print he left there by his
    grace,
His mouth, his nose, and his eyes two,
His beard, his hair, he left also.
Shield me for all that in my life
I have misdone by my wits five,
With mouth of hate and slandering,
Of false oaths and of backbiting;
For wicked boastful tongue also,
And all sins I have done and do:
Lord of heaven, forgive thou me,
Through sight of thy face that here I see.

THE KNIFE OF CIRCUMCISION

THIS knife betokens circum-
    cision,
Thus he destroyed all trans-
    gression,
Of Adam, who our sin began,
Whereby we take our stamp of
    man;
From tempting of impurity
Be my succour when I shall die.

THE PELICAN

THE Pelican his blood did
    bleed,
Therewith his nestlings for to
    feed.
This tokeneth how on the Rood
Our Lord us nourished with
    his blood,
When he did rescue us from hell,
In joy and bliss with him to dwell,
To be our Father and our food,
And we his childer meek and good.

THE THIRTY PENCE

THE Pence also that Judas told,
For which Lord Jesu Christ
    was sold,
Shield us from reason and
    avarice,
Therein to fall not anywise.

THE LANTERN

THE Lantern where they bare
    the light,
When Christ was taken in the
    night,
May it light me from nightly
    sin,
That I be never taken therein.

THE SWORDS AND STAVES

SWORDS and Staves that they
    did bear,
Of which our Jesu might have
    fear,
From friends, good Lord, pre-
    serve they me,
Of them afeard that I not be.

THE REEDS

CHRIST was stricken with a
    Reed,
Wherewith the Jews did break
    his head;
He suffered all in meekest mood,
With patient mien he silent
    stood:
When I do wrong or wrong sustain,
Grant pardon, Lord, by this thy pain.

THE HAND OF THE SMITER

THE Hand, O Lord, that tore
    thine hair,
The Hand that smote thee on
    the ear,
Be its sore smart my succour
    there,
When I do wrong through
    pride of ear;
And of all other sin also,
That with mine ears I have hearkened to.

THE RODS AND SCOURGES

WITH great Rods wast thou
　　sorely dashed,
And with the smarting Scourge
　　wast lashed;
Lord, grant that I thee ne'er
　　displease
By sins of sloth and idleness.

THE CROWN OF THORN

THE Crown of Thorn on thy
　　head prest,
To tear thine hair, thy skin
　　to burst;
Shield me, I pray, from hell's
　　dark pit,
That I err not by foolish wit.

THE PILLAR AND THE CORD

To the Pillar, Lord, also,
With a Rope they bound thee,
　　too:
Thy sinews from thy bones
　　did burst,
So hard 'twas drawn and
　　strained fast;
Lord, loose me from the bitter thong
Of unkind act and word of wrong.

THE FOOTSTEPS OF THE SAVIOUR

When he went forth by the Gate of Jerusalem, bearing his Cross and crowned with his Crown of Thorns; he went in this guise a full mile, letting fall red blood.

Thou bar'st thy Cross, and passed that
  day
Out at Jerusalem's gate-way;
And all thy footsteps sweet and good
Were marked by shedding of thy blood.
Thou met'st with women of Bethlehem,
And also of Jerusalem:
And they all wept thy woe to see:
But thou said'st to them openly:
" Nay, weep ye not for this my woe,
But for your children weep also:
For them indeed ye may weep sore,
And tears of salt for them outpour;
For they shall suffer torment hard
An hundred winters afterward."
Lord, may thy steps for us bring grace,
When forth we go with prayerful pace,
On pilgrimage, on horse or foot,
And all my sins do thou outroot.

THE NAILS

THE Nails through feet and
   hands two
Help they me out of sin and woe,
That I have yet in my life done,
Handled with hands, or on feet
   gone.

THE HAMMER

THE Hammer that was stern
   and great,
That drave the nails through
   hands and feet,
Be they mine aid in all my life,
If I be struck with staff or knife.

THE GALL AND VINEGAR

THE cup of Vinegar and Gall,
May it preserve me from sins
   all,
That to the soul are venom fell,
That I may shun the poison
   of hell.

THE SPONGE

When thou thirsted sore
      withal
They gave thee vinegar and
      gall;
If e'er I drank in gluttony
Forgive me, Lord, before I die.

THE SPEAR

Lord, the Spear so sharply
      ground,
That in thy heart made savage
      wound:
Quench it the sin that I have
      wrought,
Or evil that my heart has thought,
And all my foolish pride thereto,
And disobedience also.

THE LADDER

The Ladder 'gainst the Rood
      upstaid
To take thee down when thou
      wert dead,
If I be dead in any sin,
Spare Lord, that I should
      die therein.

89

THE TONGS

The Tongs that drew the sharp
    nails out,
From feet and hands with drag-
    ging stout,
And loosed thy body from the
    Tree,
May they of all my sins loose me.

THE SEPULCHRE

The Sepulchre wherein was
    laid
Thy blessed body all out-bled,
May it bring me before I die
Sorrow at heart and tears in
    eye.
Clean and spotless be mine end,
When that I to my grave wend;
So that I may on Judgement Day
Come to thy doom without affray,
And reach my bliss in company
Wherein no man shall ever die,
But dwell in joy with Jesu bright,
Where day is aye and never night,
That shall last without an end:
Now Jesu Christ us thither send! Amen.

36. THE MOTHER OF SORROWS

Sloane MS. (XVth century)

ST. JOHN speaketh:

" Mary, mother, come and see;
Thy Son is naileod n a tree
Hand and foot, he may not go,
His body is wounded all in woe.

" Thy sweet Son that thou hast borne,
To save mankind that was forlorn,
His head is wreathed in a thorn,
His blissful body is all torn !"

When he this tale began to tell,
Mary would not longer dwell,
But hied her fast to that hill,
Where Jesu his blood did spill.

Our Lady speaketh:

" My sweet Son, that art so dear,
Why have men hanged thee here ?
Thy head is wreathed in a briar;
My lovely Son, where is thy cheer ?

" Thy body that in me did rest,
Thy comely mouth that I have kissed,
Now on Rood is made thy nest;
Dear Child, what now for me were
best ?"

Jesus speaketh:

> " Woman, to John I thee betake;
> John, keep this woman for my sake;
> For sinful souls my death I take,
> On Rood I hang for man's sake.

> " This game I alone must play,
> For sinful souls I die to-day;
> There is no man that goeth by the way,
> Who of my pains can well say."

37. THE LAMENTATION OF MARY

Camb. Univ. Lib. MS. (XVth century)

OF all women that ever were born
　　That bare children, abide and see
　　How my Son lieth here forlorn,
Upon my skirt, taken from the Tree.
Your children ye dance upon your knee
　With laughing, kissing, and merry cheer:
Behold my Child, behold well me,
　For now lieth dead mine own Son dear.

O woman, woman, happy art thou;
　Thy child's cap thou castest upon;
Thou strokest his hair, beholdest his hue,
　Thou wottest not well when thou hast done.
But ever, alas, I make my moan,
　To see my Son's head as it is here;
I pick out thorns by one and one,
　For now lieth dead mine own Son dear.

O woman, a chaplet chosen thou hast,
　Thy child to wear it doth thee liking;
Thou pinnest it on; rejoice thou mayst,
　And I sit with my Son sore weeping.
His chaplet is thorns sore pricking;
　His mouth I kiss with sorrowful cheer;
I sit weeping and then siking,*
　For now lieth dead mine own Son dear.

* sighing

93

38. SEE WHAT CHRIST SUFFERED FOR OUR SAKE

Lambeth MS. (c. 1430)

BOTH young and old, whiche'er ye be,
　　In Jesu's name good cheer ye make,
　　Lift up your hearts, behold, and see
What Christ hath suffered for our sake.
As meek as any lamb was he,
　　We may of him example take,
And suffer too in our degree,
　　And in his service ever walk.

And if our friends forsake us here,
　　So that we be left all alone,
Think we on him that bought us dear,
　　And to him make we all our moan.
For of that Lord well may we hear
　　What wrongs he bore, his foes among,
When his disciples fled for fear,
　　And only Mary stayed and John.

If any wrong to us be wrought,
　　Be it in word or else in deed,
Be of good hope and bear in thought
　　How God may help us all at need.
And think how Jesu Christ us bought,
　　And for our sins his blood would bleed:
Since his own guilt was less than nought,
　　For ne'er did he a sinful deed.

94

If wicked men do us defame,
   Then think how Christ was bought and
      sold;
For him to suffer is no shame,
   But in his service be we bold.
Or if men injure our good name,
   We must forgive, both young and old;
For though we suffer cruel blame,
   Christ suffered more a thousand-fold.

Of poverty if we complain,
   Because we lack some worldly good,
Think we on Christ, our Sovereign,
   How poor he hung upon the Rood,
And how he strived not again,
   But e'er was meek and mild of mood;
To follow him we should be fain,
   In what degree soe'er we stood.

Though sorrow be on every side,
   And all about us wrong and woe,
Yet suffer meekly and abide
   Even as he endured also;
For he too was in full great dread,
   When to his Passion he should go;
He suffered more in his manhood
   Than e'er did man, or e'er shall do.

39. A MOURNING SONG OF THE LOVE OF GOD

Bodleian MS. (XVth century)

JESU, I now begin
  To love thee day and night;
  From earth my soul to wean
I shall do all my might.
Jesu, that know'st not sin,
Didst in a maid alight;
'Twas all my love to win
Jesu became my Knight.

My Leman is full true
Of love and full steadfast;
Each day beginneth new
Love that is never past.
I would that all him knew
And on him their love cast;
Sure none of them would rue,
Neither the first nor last.

My Leman is so meek,
So mild, so sweet, so still;
Full gentle too in speech,
Upbraid he never will;

96

Remembering good of each,
Forgetting each man's ill;
If I flee, he will seek;
His love is with me still.

Although without he stand,
Calling before my gate,
Till frozen is foot and hand,
As tied unto a stake,
He takes nor staff nor wand
With wrath me for to wake;
My love binds him with band,
And nought shall his love shake.

My Leman hath so spread
His arms that are so long,
That I am nothing dread,
For his hand is full strong.
When I was from him fled
On him he took the wrong;
Till he to death was bled,
For my love there he hung.

All other I shall forsake,
And put from out my thought;
To thee, Jesu, I me take,
So dear thou hast me bought.
All other love will make
Ending, and wax to nought;
Thy love I'll not forsake,
For that brings us aloft.

Jesu, my Leman sweet,
That hast died on the Tree,
With all my might I thee beseech,
By thy wounds two and three,
That as deep into mine heart
May thy love fastened be,
As was the spear into thine heart,
When thou suffredst death for me !

40. O VOS OMNES QUI TRANSITIS

Harley MS. (end of XIVth century)

YE that this way do pass,
Bide, and behold my face !
And look if any woe or pine
May be likened unto mine !

41. HIS COMING

Harley MS. (end of XIVth century)

WHO is he that comes so bright,
With bloody garments all be-
dight ?

He is both God and man,
Such was never seen before.
For Adam's sin is Jesu dead,
And therefore is his robe so red !

42. CHRIST ON THE CROSS

Harley MS. (end of XIVth century).

WHOSO sees him on the Rood,
    Jesu, his loved One,
    While his mother by him stood
Sore weeping, and Saint John,
With his side pierced sore
For love of thee, O man,
Well should he his sins forsake,
Tears shed, and amends make,
As of love he can !

43. A SONG OF THE PASSION

Egerton MS. (c. 1300)

SUMMER'S here and winter's gone,
  Days grow bright and long,
  And the birds now every one
Glad their hearts with song.
I alone am sad and drear,
In earth's joy I have no cheer;
    'Tis for a little Child,
    That is so mild,
        And dear.

This Child that is so rich and mild,
And eke of noble mien,
Hath sought me long in wood and wild,
Where bank and bush is green,
Sought me, until at last he found,
All for one poor apple bound.
    What brake my thong
    So stout and strong?
        His wound.

This Child that is so rich and bold
Bent him low for me,
To the Jews for me was sold,
Nought to them was he.
Said they in their savage mood:
  " Let us nail him to the Rood;
    But first his name
    Mock we with shame
        And blood."

This Child, Jesu is his name,
Is King of all the earth;
Him they put to bitter shame,
Him they made their mirth;
Then upon a ghastly Tree
Wounds they gave him two and three,
  Set bitter drink
   To his lip's brink:
    'Twas for me !

There the Maiden-Mother stood,
Mary, full of grace:
Bitter tears, yea, tears of blood,
Shed she in that place.
From Christ dript the saving rain,
Changed he was in limb and mien;
  As the prey
   The hunters slay,
    Was he slain.

Death he suffered, our sweet Friend,
High upon the Rood.
For our sins he made amend
By his saving blood.
Therewithal he did descend,
And the keep of limbo rend,
  And set free there
   Whoever were
    Pure and good.

He rose up on the third day,
And sat him on his throne,
And he shall come on Doomsday,
To judge us every one.
With many a tear and many a cry
The lawless man alone will die;
    But grant with him
    That we may climb
      On high !

44. THE VIRGIN'S COMPLAINT

Lambeth MS. (c. 1430)

AS reason ruled my reckless mind,
    By wild ways as I wandering went,
    A solemn city I chanced to find;
To turn thereto was my intent.
A Maiden I met, a Mother kind,
Sobbing and sighing without relent;
She wept, she wailed, so sore she pined;
Her hair and face she tore and rent;
She rent and tore with great torment,
She scarred her skin, both body and breast;
She said these words as ever she went:
    " *Filius regis mortuus est.*"

" The King's Son," said she, " is dead,
The joy, the substance of my life;
It pierced, to see my Son so bleed,
My mother's heart as with a knife.
My Son that I was wont to feed,
To lull, to lap with songs rife;
That he his own heart's blood should
    shed,
Maketh me, his mother, in much strife.
I am both maiden, mother, and wife,
And sons have no more to feed at my breast;
I must make sorrow without relief,
    For *Filius regis mortuus est.*

" This King's Son, mine own dear Child,
Hangs on the Cross; I stand and see
How he is wounded and defiled
With spitting and spears so piteously.
I cried upon him as I were wild,
' My sweet dear Son, seest thou not me,
Thine own dear mother?' Then he me
　　beheld,
And said, ' Mourn not, mother; thy sorrow
　　let be;
I shall be thine, and come to thee.'
He spake, he swooned, and never ceased.
Ah, Son mine, Son mine, upon the Tree !
　　　Filius regis mortuus est.

" He dieth, he dieth who is my bliss;
He swooned, he died; I cried ' Alas !'
No wonder I go in heaviness !
My Father, my Brother, my Spouse he
　　was,
My Mother, my succour, and all that is.
Now fatherless and motherless I may forth
　　pass,
Brotherless, spouseless, full wretched i-wis,
As a thing forsaken, that nothing has.
Ah, Gabriel, thou callest me full of
　　grace;
Nay, full of sorrow thou now me seest;
The tears trickle down upon my face,
　　　For *Filius regis mortuus est.*

" I looked up," she said, "unto my Child;
I cried on the Jews, and bade them hang
The mother by the Son that ne'er was
    defiled.
O death, death, thou dost me wrong;
My Babe thou slew'st, that never was
    wild:
Come, slay the mother. Why tarriest thou
    so long ?
Thou murderer, why art thou now so mild
Unto the mother, that unto death would
    belong ?
Thou rackest my Son with pains strong:
Rack then the mother at her request.
Alas, I may sing a sorrowful song,
      That *Filius regis mortuus est !*

" Ah, thou earth, on thee I claim appeal,
That thou receivedst his innocent blood !
Thou stone, why wouldst thou be so frail,
To be the mortice whereon his Cross
    stood ?
He made the earth and the stones to feel,
And ye are the ministers now to the Rood
To slay your Maker. Ye know full well
He never did evil, but evermore good.
He ever was meek and mild of mood;
Now is he pierced as it were a beast.
Alas, my Babe, my one life's Food,
      Filius regis mortuus est !

" Thou Tree, thou Cross, how durst thou be
A gallows to hang thy Maker so ?
To his Father he may accuse thee
That wouldst be cause of his Son's woe:
Not cause, but help that he slain should be.
Ye trees, cry mercy; ye are my foe;
Had ye been ordained a rood for me,
To hang me by him, it had been well so.
But where shall I turn, or whither go ?
The Tree hath hanged a King, a Priest:
Of all kings is none other so,
　　　As *Filius regis mortuus est.*

" Ye creatures unkind ! Thou steel and sharp
　　thorn !
How durst ye slay your best Friend,
The holiest Child that ever was born ?
Ye have him wounded, ye have him pined:
Spear and nail his body have worn.
Thou spear, why sufferedst thou the smith
　　thee to grind
So sharp that all his heart thou hast out-torn ?
I may cry out on thee both even and morn.
A Maiden's blameless Son hast thou opprest.
I wring and weep as a thing forlorn.
　　　Filius regis mortuus est.

" Yea, dead is he, my fair Lord !
Now dead is my dear Child, alas !
Now may I walk in this world
As a wretch that wanteth grace.

And this I say to bear record:
No more may I look upon his face;
Thus I come from Calvary-ward,
Weeping and wailing that I born was.
If any man love me, let him give me a place,
Where I may weep my fill, and rest,
And my Son will grant him a place that he has:
  Filius regis mortuus est !"

45. FRAGMENT OF A MEDITATION OF ST AUGUSTINE

Bodleian MS. (early XIVth century)

WHITE was his hallowed breast,
　　And red of blood his side,
　　Livid his fair hands,
His wounds deep and wide.

Stark were his naked arms,
　　Wide-spread upon the Rood;
From five wounds in his body
　　Streams ran of blood!

46. DIALOGUE BETWEEN CHRIST AND OUR LADY

Digby MS. (c. 1275)

" STAND well, Mother, under the Rood;
Behold thy Child with gladsome mood;
Mother, blithe may'st thou be ! "
" Son, how may I blithe stand ?
I see thy dear feet and thine hand,
Nailed to the cruel Tree."

" Mother, do away thy weeping,
I suffer death for all mankind;
Guilt of mine own is none."
" Son, 'tis I feel thy death-wound;
That sword is at mine heart's ground,
Whereof foretold me Simeon."

" Mother, do away thy tears:
Wipe thou away thy bloody tears:
They rack me worse than death ! "
" Son, how may I my tears staunch ?
I see thy bloody wounds drench
From thy heart to thy feet."

" Mother, I may no longer dwell;
The time is come I go to hell.
I suffer this for thy sake."
" Son, have I thy mercy found ?
I die almost; I fall to ground:
So sorrowful death was never none ! "

47. THE HOURS OF THE CROSS
York Minster MS. (*XVth century*)

LORD, undo my lips, Jesu, heaven's
King,
      And my mouth shall so all thy praises
sing.

MATINS

God and man at morning-tide
                  He was taken,
And of all his earthly friends
                  Left forsaken.
To the Jews betrayed and sold,
And cast into the bitter hold.
Lord, by the pain thou didst suffer at early
      morn,
Let not my soul on thy Judgement Day be
      forlorn.

PRIME

At Prime was Jesus unto Pilate led,
      They bound him as a thief, and nought he
      said.
False witnesses on this side and on that
Scoff'd, and upon God's holy visage spat.
Lord, by each shame thou didst suffer at
      hour of Prime,
Let not my soul be ashamed at thy judgement
      time.

TIERCE

At time of Tierce there rang a cry and call;
For mockery they clad him in a purple pall,
And set upon his head a golden crown
withal,
And on his back they laid a bitter Cross
and tall.
Lord, by each shame thou didst suffer in that
place,
To be shriven of deadly sin give me thy grace.

SEXT

At time of mid-day they bound him to the
Rood
Betwixt two robbers that had spilt many
men's blood.
To sate his bitter thirst they gave him
bitter drink,
Mingled gall and vinegar unto his lips'
brink.
Lord, by each shame thou didst suffer and
each fell gash,
Save us, we pray, from our foes, the world
the fiend, and the flesh.

NONE

At the time of None Jesu uplift a moan,
And gave his soul to the hand of his Father
upon the throne.

A soldier smote his God to the heart, and
knew no ruth,
And gloom waxed deep at the death of
him that was God in truth.
As out of thy side, O Lord, ran down the
fair red blood
Lave us, O Lord, in that stream; let our
ransom be thy blood !

VESPERS

At the time of Evensong they took him from
the Rood,
Him that was mighty Godhead, so gracious
and so good,
Lord, let thy healing pains and the shedding of thy blood
Be unto us our nourishment and ghostly
food.
Lord, by each shame thou didst suffer at
evening hour,
Let not my soul be thrall to Satan's deadly
power.

COMPLINE

At the hour of Compline they laid him in
the grave,
The noble body of Jesu, that came to save;
With spicery he was buried, as Scripture
saith;
'Tis he shall save us from hell; think we
sadly upon his death.

O blessed Christ, these hours canonical,
To thee I offer with meek devotion;
For us thou sufferedst these sorrows all.
So by remembrance of thy Passion
Make me, according as thy mercy is,
Partaker of thy crown and endless bliss !

PART THE FOURTH
OF OUR LADY

48. INVOCATION OF OUR LADY

Chaucer's Prioress's Tale (end of XIVth century)

O MOTHER Maid! O Maid and
Mother free!
O bush unburnt, burning in Moses'
sight!
That down didst ravish from the Deity,
  Through humbleness, the spirit that did
  alight
  Upon thy heart, whence, through that
  glory's might,
Conceived was the Father's sapience,
Help me to tell it in thy reverence!

Lady, thy goodness, thy magnificence,
  Thy virtue, and thy great humility,
Surpass all science and all utterance;
  For sometimes, Lady, ere men pray to
  thee,
  Thou go'st before in thy benignity,
The light to us vouchsafing of thy prayer,
To be our guide unto thy Son so dear.

My knowledge is so weak, O blissful Queen,
   To tell abroad thy mighty worthiness,
That I the weight of it may not sustain;
   But as a child of twelve months old, or less,
   That laboureth his language to express,
Even so fare I; and therefore I thee pray,
Guide thou my song, which I of thee shall
   say.

49. ECCE ANCILLA DOMINI

Camb. Univ. Lib. MS. (XVth century)

SAID the virgin without vice,
　　When Gabriel her greet graciously,
　　That holy pinnacle of great price—
" Of thee shall spring a full sweet
　　spice;"
Then said the maiden full mildly,
" And since I am so little of price,
　　　Ecce Ancilla Domini."

" Hail be thou, gracious, without guilt,
Mary, of all most blest;
Within thy body shall be fulfilled
As all the prophets do attest.
God will be born within thy breast."
Then said the maiden full mildly,
" To me he shall be a welcome Guest;
　　　Ecce Ancilla Domini."

But when she saw an angel bright,
She was afear'd in all her thought,
And at his speech well wonder she
　　might.
Then said the angel, " Dread thee not;

A blissful tiding I have thee brought."
Then said the maiden full mildly,
" As God will so be it wrought;
    Ecce Ancilla Domini."

The angel said, " Conceive thou shalt
Within thy body bright
A Child that Jesu shall be called,
That is great God's Son of might.
Thou art his tabernacle dight."
Then said the maiden full mildly,
" Since he said never against right,
    Ecce Ancilla Domini."

" Call him Jesus of Nazareth,
God and man in one degree;
He as man shall suffer death,
And reign in David's dignity;
A blissful word he sends to thee."
Then said the maiden full mildly,
" He shall be welcome unto me;
    Ecce Ancilla Domini.

" But with man I never met;
Now, lord, how shall I go with child ?"
Then said the angel that her greet,
" With none such shalt thou be defiled;
The Holy Ghost will in thee build."
Then said the maiden full mildly,
" As God will so be it done;
    Ecce Ancilla Domini."

When the angel was vanished away,
She stood in study all in her thought,
And to herself she did say,
" All God's will shall be wrought,
For he is wisest of all wit,
As witnesseth well his story."
At that word the knot was knit.
   " *Ecce Ancilla Domini.*"

50. ALMA REDEMPTORIS MATER

Trin. Coll. Camb. MS. (XVth century)

AS I lay upon a night,
My thought was on a Lady bright,
That men call Mary of might,
Redemptoris Mater.

To her came Gabriel so bright,
And said, " Hail, Mary, full of might,
Favour hast thou in God's sight,
Redemptoris Mater."

Right as the sun shineth in glass,
So Jesu in his mother was,
And thereby wit men that she was
Redemptoris Mater.

Now is born that Babe of bliss,
And Queen of Heaven his mother is,
And therefore think me that she is
Redemptoris Mater.

After to heaven he took his flight,
And there he sits with his Father of might,
With him is crowned that Lady bright,
Redemptoris Mater.

51. THE ROSE-TREE

Richard Hill's Commonplace Book, Balliol
MS. (c. 1520)

O F a rose, a lovely rose,
　　And of a rose I sing a song !

Hearken to me both old and young,
How a rose began to spring,
A fairer rose to my liking
Sprang there never in King's land.

Six branches are on that tree seen,
They be both bright and sheen;
The rose is Mary, heaven's Queen,
Of her bosom a blossom sprung.

The first branch was of great might;
It sprung on Christmas night.
The star shone over Bethlehem bright,
That men might see both broad and long.

The second branch was of great honour;
It was sent from heaven's bower.
Blessed be that fair flower,
It shall break the bonds of sin !

The third branch wide spread,
Where Mary lay in bed;
The bright beam three kings led
To Bethlehem where that branch they
　　found.

The fourth branch sprang into hell,
The boast of Satan for to fell;
There might no soul therein dwell.
Blest be the time that branch 'gan spring !

The fifth branch was fair in foot;
It sprang to heaven, both top and root,
There to dwell and be our boot,
And yet 'tis seen in priest's hands !

The sixth branch by-and-by,
It is the five joys of mild Mary;
Now Christ save all this company,
And send us good life and long !

52. AD BEATAM VIRGINEM

Hoccleve, Bodleian MS. (early XVth century)

MOTHER of God and Virgin un-
defiled;
O blissful Queen, of all queens
Emperice;
Pray for thy child that is in sore sin soiled,
To God thy Son, the punisher of vice,
That of his mercy, though I be unwise
And negligent in keeping of his law,
His high grace may my soul unto him draw.

Mother of mercy, way of indulgence,
That of all virtue art superlative,
Saver of us by thy benevolence,
O humble Lady, mother and maid and wife,
Causer of peace, stayer of woe and strife,
My prayer unto thy dear Son represent,
Since for my guilt I fully me repent.

Benignant comforter of wretches all,
Be at mine ending, when that I shall die.
O well of pity, unto thee I call,
Fount of all sweetness, help me to defy
The bitter fiend, that will for ever try
With all his might to pluck at the balance
To weigh us down—keep us from his
nuisance.

And, for thou art ensample of chastity,
And of all virgins worship and honour,
Among all women blessed may thou be.
Now speak and pray thou to our Saviour,
That he me send such grace and such favour,
That all the heat of burning lechery
He quench in me, O blessed maid Mary!

O blessed Lady, thou clear light of day,
Temple of God, and root of all goodness,
That by thy prayers wipest clean away
The filth of all our sinful wickedness,
Put forth thine hand and succour my distress,
And from temptation deliver me
Of wicked thought through thy benignity.

Thou art the way of our redemption,
For Christ of thee hath deigned for to take
Flesh and eke blood for this intention,
Upon a Cross to suffer for our sake.
His precious death made all the fiends to
  quake,
And Christian people to rejoice for ever;
Help that we never from his grace dissever.

Well ought we thee to worship and honour,
Palace of Christ, flower of virginity;
Since upon thee was laid the charge and cure
To bear the Lord of heaven and earth and sea,
And all created things that therein be.
Of heaven's King thou art predestinate
To heal our spirits of their sick estate.

The gates of Paradise were oped by thee,
And broken were the portals eke of hell.
By thee a world restored anew we see.
Of all virtue thou art the spring and well.
By thee all bounty, shortly for to tell,
In heaven and earth by thine own ordinance
Performed is, our spirits' sustenance.

Apostle and familiar friend of Christ,
The chosen virgin whom he loved, Saint John,
Shining Apostle and Evangelist,
And best beloved among them every one,
I pray thee, with our Lady dear be one,
And unto Jesu Christ for us all pray:
Do so for us, Christ's darling, as I say!

Mary and John, jewels of heaven twain,
O twin lamps, shining in the bright presence
Of our Lord God, now do your busy pain
To wash away the clouds of our offence,
That we may so make steadfast resistance
Against the fiend, and make him to bewail
That your prayers unto God have such avail.

Be ye our help and our protection,
Since by the merit of your virginity,
The privilege of his election
God did confirm in you, upon a Tree
Hanging, and unto one of you said He,
Right in this wise, as I rehearse can:
" Behold here, lo, this is thy son, woman."

And to the other: " Here thy mother, lo."
Then pray I thee that by the great sweetness
Of the high love that God betwixt you two
With his mouth made, and by his nobleness
Hath you conjoined through his blissfulness
As mother and son, help us in all our need,
And for our sins make thou our hearts to
   bleed.

Unto you twain do I my soul commend,
Mary and John, for my salvation.
And help me that I may my life amend.
And grant now that the habitation
Of the Holy Ghost, our recreation,
Dwell in my heart this day and evermore,
And of my soul God wash away the sore!
   Amen.

53. A PRAYER TO THE VIRGIN

Egerton MS. (c. 1300)

BLESSED be thou, Lady, full of
  heaven's bliss,
  Sweet flower of Paradise, mother of
gentleness;
Pray to thy Son, Jesu Christ, that by guidance of his,
Where'er on earth I may be, his love I never
  may miss.

To thee, fair Lady, mine orison will I begin.
The love of thy dear sweet Son do thou teach
  me to win;
Full oft I sigh and sorrow, and make no end
  of my teen,
But thou in thy mercy, Lady, bring me out
  of my sin.

Oft I cry for thy mercy, and oft on thy sweet
  name call;
My flesh is foul, the world is false, look thou
  that I ne'er fall.
Lady meek, do thou shield me from pains
  of hell,
And bring me into that bliss that tongue may
  never tell.

Bright and fair Queen of Heaven, pray for
    me to him thou bore;
The sins that I have done I rue them now full
    sore;
Full oft have I thee forsaken, but I will never
    more,
Lady, for thy dear sake, trust to the devil's
    lore.

Blessed be thou, Lady, my sweet fair friend,
And pray Jesu Christ, thy Son, that he me
    send,
That wheresoe'er upon earth I be, I hence
    may wend
And dwell in his Paradise for ever without
    an end !

54. THE SONG OF WILLIAM OF SHOREHAM

Brit. Mus. MS. (XVth century)

MARY, maid, mild and free,
Chamber of the Trinity,
  List awhile to me,
As I thee greet with song;
  Though my feet unclean be,
Help me amend my wrong.

Thou art Queen of Paradise,
Of heaven, of earth, of all that is;
  Thou barest the King of bliss
Without or stain or sore;
  Thou hast set right that was amiss,
Saved that was lost before.

Thou art the dove of Noe,
That brought the branch of olive-tree,
  As token that peace should be
Between God and man.
  Sweet Lady, help thou me,
When I have lived my span.

Take, Lady, this little song,
That out of sinful heart sprong.
  Against the fiend make me strong;
To me thy guidance lend,
  And though I have done bitter wrong,
Grant me to amend.

55. ROSA MYSTICA

Trin. Coll. Camb. MS. (XVth century)

THERE is no rose of such virtue
As the rose that bare Jesu.
Alleluia.

For in this rose contained was
Heaven and earth in little space.
Res miranda !

By that rose we may well see
There is one God in Persons three.
Pares forma.

The angels sang, the shepherds too:
Gloria in Excelsis Deo ;
Gaudeamus !

Leave we all this worldly mirth,
And follow we this joyful birth;
Transeamus !

56. I SING OF A MAIDEN

Sloane MS. (XVth century)

I SING of a maiden
Of matchless fame:
King of all kings
Was her Son that came.

He came all so still
Where his mother was,
As dew in April
That falls on the grass.

He came all so still
To his mother's bower,
As dew in April
That falls on the flower.

He came all so still
Where his mother lay,
As dew in April
That forms on the spray.

Mother and maiden
Was none but she;
Well may such a Lady
God's mother be !

133

57. HAIL, BLESSED MARY
Lambeth MS. (*c.* 1430)

HAIL to thee, Mary, the mother of
   Christ,
  Blest above all that ever bare child;
Thou that didst blithely conceive in thy breast
 God's very Son, so meek and so mild !
Hail, sweet maiden and undefiled,
Wellspring and source of all wisdom !
 Fairer than flower of the woodland wild,
  Ave Regina Coelorum !

Hail, comely Queen, thou comfort in care;
 Hail, blessed Lady, so pure and bright;
Hail, thou sainer of every sore;
 Hail, thou lamp with beaming light !
 Blissful maid, in whom Christ was pight,★
Joy thou of mortals every one;
 Pinnacle thou of heaven's height,
  Mater Regis Angelorum !

Hail, crowned Queen, fairest of all;
 Hail, thou that didst our blitheness breed;
Thou, on whom poor women call
 In child-bearing sore bestead !
 Hail, thou that all the fiends do dread,
And shall do till the day of doom;
 With maid's milk thou thy Son hast fed,
  O Maria Flos Virginum !

★ Fixed.

134

Hail, thou goodly ground of grace;
　　Hail, blest star upon the sea;
Comfort thou in every case;
　　Chiefest thou of charity !
　　Well of wisdom and mercy;
Mother of Jesu, God's own Son;
　　Hail, tabernacle of the Trinity,
　　　　Funde preces ad Filium !

Hail to thee, Virgin of virgins;
　　Hail, blessed mother, blessed maid,
That didst nourish sweet Jesu;
　　Hail, of all chastity the head !
Lady, so keep us in our last day,
　　That to thy kingdom we may come;
For me and all true Christians pray
　　　　Pro salute fidelium.　Amen !

58. THREE LITTLE PRAYERS TO OUR LADY

Lambeth MS. (c. 1430)

1

HAIL to thee, O Mary, Christ's own mother dear,
Queen of Heaven art thou, fair and sweet of cheer;
Star of Heaven art thou, shining bright and clear,
Help me, Lady, full of might, and my prayer hear !
Ave Maria !

2

Hail, blessed Mary, heaven's Queen so meek,
Blessed be thy name, yea, good it is to speak;
To thee, Lady, I make my moan; my voice do thou hear,
That of the seven deadly sins I may die clear !
Ave Maria !

3

Hail to thee, Mary upon thy throne;
Prithee, sweet Lady, grant me my boon !
Let me love Jesu, and my life amend,
And bring me to bliss that never shall end !
Ave Maria !

136

59. A SONG TO THE VIRGIN

Egerton MS. (c. 1300)

O THOU that art so fair and bright,
   Velut maris stella,
Brighter than the day is light,
   Parens et puella,
I cry to thee; look thou to me;
Lady, pray thy Son for me,
   Tam pia,
So that I may come to thee,
   Maria !

Thou in care art counsel best,
   Felix fecundata ;
To the weary thou art rest,
   Mater honorata.
Pray thy Son in gentle mood,
That for us all shed his blood,
   In Cruce,
That we all may come to him
   In luce !

This our world was all forlorn,
   Eva peccatrice ;
Till the day our Lord was born,
   De te genitrice.

137   F

With *Ave* there went away
Darkest night, and comes the day
    Salutis,
And from thee springs forth the well
    Virtutis !

Lady, flower of every thing,
    Rosa sine spina,
That bore Jesu, heaven's King,
    Gratia divina.
Thou of all dost bear the prize,
Lady, Queen of Paradise,
    Electa ;
Maiden mild, that mother now
    Es effecta !

Well he knows he is thy Son,
    Ventre quem portasti,
He will grant thee every boon,
    Parvum quem lactasti.
So kind and so good he is,
He hath brought us all to bliss
    Superni,
And hath shut up the foul pit
    Inferni !

60. GAUDE FLORE VIRGINALI

D. T. Mylle, Lambeth MS. (c. 1430)

HAIL, Flower of all virginity,
In heaven thou hast priority
    Of worship and honour;
Thy bliss is more in dignity
Than all the saints that e'er may be,
    Or angels in heaven's tower !

Hail, that art God's spouse so dear,
Ne'er was sunny day so clear,
    Nor of so great a light;
There may never sun shine here
As thou dost in heaven appear
    With beams that are so bright !

Hail, vessel of virtue and grace,
Crowned Queen in that high place
    Where thy Son is King !
Angels all in his presence
Are under thine obedience,
    And do thee worshipping !

Hail, O mother-maiden free,
Through the bond of charity
    To God so wholly knit,
That whate'er thine asking be
All the Holy Trinity
    Gladly grants thee it !

Hail, O fruit of every flower,
Whosoe'er doth thee honour
　With prayer, night or day,
God our Father, paying heed,
Granteth gladly to their meed
　Bliss that lasteth aye !

Hail, mother of Christ Jesu,
Full of grace and of virtue,
　That for thy holiness
So high art now in dignity !
Thou sittest next the Trinity
　In great honour and bliss !

Hail, O spotless maiden pure;
Rest thou evermore secure,
　That these thy joys seven
Never shall grow less or cease,
But for evermore increase,
　While God reigns in heaven !

61. REGINA COELI

Bodleian MS. (XVth century)

QUEEN of Heaven, make thou mirth,
    And praise God with all thy might,
    For of thee he took his birth,
That is health and life and light.
He rose from death, as promised he;
    Save us, God, when need is most.
Pray for us the Trinity,
    Father, Son, and Holy Ghost !

62. THE WONDER

*Richard Hill's Common-place Book, Balliol
    MS. (c. 1520)*

WIT is a-wonder, and reason out-ran,
    How maid is mother, and God is
        man.
Leave thy search, and believe the wonder;
God is the Lord, and skill goeth under !

63. THE SECOND EVE

Harley MS. (end of XIVth century)

THE gates of Paradise
　　Were shut and locked right fast;
Our Lady did arise,
And threw them wide at last !

64. A SONG OF MARY, GOD'S MOTHER

Harley MS. (end of XIVth century)

JESU, my sweet Son, most dear,
　On bed full poor thou liest here,
　　And that me grieveth sore.
Thy cradle is a manger bare,
That the ox and ass may share,
　Well may I weep therefore.
Jesu sweet, be nothing wroth,
Though I have nor clout nor cloth
　In which thee to fold.
No cloth nor clout thee in to fold
Have I; but in my bosom rest,
Lay thou thy feet against my breast,
　And shield thee from the cold !

65. THE FIVE JOYS OF OUR LADY

Bodleian MS. (XVth century)

MARY, for the love of thee
    Glad and merry shall we be;
    We shall sing unto thee
        Tua quinque gaudia.

The first joy that came to thee
Was when the angel greeted thee,
And said, " Mary, full of charity,
        Ave, plena gratia !"

The second joy that was full good
Was when God's Son took flesh and blood;
Without sorrow or change of mood
        Enixa es puerpera.

The third joy was full of might:
'Twas when God's Son on Rood was pight,
Dead and buried and laid in sight,
        Surrexit die tertia.

The fourth joy was on that Thursday,
When God to heaven took his way,
God and man without a nay,
        Ascendit supra sidera.

143

The fifth joy is for to come,
At the dreadful day of doom,
When he shall judge us all and some
            Ad coeli palatia.

Mary to serve God give us grace,
And greet her with joys in every place,
To come before her Son's face,
            In saeculorum saecula !

66. THE ANNUNCIATION

Bodleian MS. (XVth century)

TIDINGS true there be come new, sent
from the Trinity,
By Gabriel to Nazareth, city of Galilee;
A clean maiden and pure Virgin, through her
humility
Conceived the second Person in divinity.

When he first presented was before her fair
visage,
In most demure and goodly wise he did to
her homage,
And said, " Lady, from heaven so high, that
high Lord's heritage,
Who of thee born would be, I am sent on
message !

" Hail, Virgin celestial, the meekest that
ever was;
Hail, temple of divinity and mirror of all
grace;
Hail, Virgin pure, I thee ensure within a little
space
Thou shalt receive and him conceive that
shall bring great solace."

Suddenly she, abashed truly, but not a whit
    dismayed,
With mind discreet and meek spirit unto
    the angel said,
" By what manner should I a child bear,
    who, ever a maid,
Have lived chaste all my life past, and never
    man assayed ?"

Then again to her certain answered the angel,
" O Lady dear, be of good cheer, and terror
    never feel;
Thou shalt conceive in thy body, maiden,
    very God himself,
In whose birth heaven and earth shall joy,
    called Emmanuel.

" Mark this," he said, " six months past
    thy cousin Elizabeth
That was barren, conceived Saint John, true
    is it that I tell;
Since she in age, why not in youth mayst
    thou conceive as well,
If God's will be, to whose high power all
    things are possible ?"

Then again to the angel she answered
    womanly,
" Whatever my Lord command me do, I
    will obey meekly,
Ecce sum humillima ancilla Domini,
Secundum verbum tuum," she said, *"fiat mihi."*

PART THE FIFTH

OF THE FOUR LAST THINGS

67. THE THREE CARES

Richard Hill's Common-place Book, Balliol
MS. (c. 1520)

WHEN I think on thinges three,
    Well careful may I be:
    One is, that I shall hen;*
Another is, I wot not when.
Of the third is my most care,
For I shall dwell I wot not where.
Man! remember whence thou come and
    where thou shalt;
And to thy fellow-Christian do no wrong;
    For man without mercy, of mercy shall
      miss;
    And he shall have mercy, that merciful is.

* Hence.

68. THIS WORLD'S JOY

Harley MS. (*c.* 1300)

WINTER wakens all my care,
Now the trees are black and bare;
Oft I sigh in dark despair,
When it cometh to my thought
How this world's joy goes all to nought.

Now it is, and now no more,
As though it ne'er had been before;
True the word declared of yore:
    " Sure abides God's will alone ":
Die we must, for all our moan.

All that grew in gladsome weather,
Fadeth, flower and leaf together;
We shall pass, we know not whither.
    Jesu, lead us by the hand
    To thine ever-summer land !

69. DIES IRAE

William of Nassington, Thornton MS. (*c.* 1440)

LORD, at thy dreadful day of doom,
        When thou shalt from thy heaven come
        With all thine angels bright and clear,
With thine Apostles and saints so dear,
In the same form of human birth
Wherein thou guiltless died on earth,
The good and evil of all lands
To judge, with scars in feet and hands,
Which thou didst bear for sinful men—
What shall I do or say, Lord, then,
When all our works that e'er we did
Shall be made plain, and nought be hid?
Whereof account we all shall give,
And judged be as we did live;
And I with me no good shall bring
Before so high a Judge and King,
But sins that are so manifold,
That they should ne'er by tongue be told;
I am in woe and dread therefore,
Needs must I quake with trembling sore,
Then shall I find nor plea nor plan,
Save only David's, holy man—
" Do thou, Lord, with thy servant vile
After thy saving mercy deal;
And into judgement come thou not
With me, thy child, whom thou hast bought.

For great dread hath my heart alway
Of doom, and dread will not away."
For surely mercy none gets he,
That in this life turns not to thee;
And none shall in that day be safe,
Save in his life he mercy have.
For thou of mercy art liberal,
To grant it both to great and small.
So, Lord, since aye it is thy plan
To give thy mercy to each man,
That seeks it while on earth he live;
Such grace in life do thou me give,
To turn to thee and flee from sin,
That I may here thy mercy win,
Whereby I shall on that dread day
Be led to bliss that lasteth aye ! Amen.

70. PULVIS IN PULVEREM

Lambeth MS. (c. 1430)

*W*HEN *life is most loved, and death
        is most hated ;
     Then doth death draw his draught,
and maketh man full naked.*

Earth out of earth is wonderfully wrought,
Earth of earth hath gotten a dignity of
    nought.
Earth upon earth hath set all his thought,
How that earth upon earth may be high
    brought.

Earth upon earth would be a king,
But how earth to earth shall turn, thinks he
    ne'er a thing;
When that earth shall bid earth home his
    rents bring,
Then shall earth from earth have a pitiful
    parting.

Earth upon earth winneth castles and towers ;
Then earth saith to earth: " All is now ours."
When earth upon earth hath builded up his
    bowers,
Then shall earth upon earth suffer sharp
    showers.

153

Earth goeth upon earth as mould upon
 mould,
So goeth earth upon earth all glittering in
 gold;
As though earth unto earth again never
 should;
And yet shall earth back to earth sooner than
 he would.

O thou wretched earth that on earth travail-
 est night and day,
To broider the earth, and paint the earth
 with wanton array;
Yet shall thou, earth, for all thy earth, make
 thou it never so quaint and gay,
Out of this earth into the earth, there to
 cling as a clot of clay.

O wretched man, why art thou proud, that
 art of the earth taked?
Hither broughtest thou no shroud, but poor
 came thou and naked;
When thy soul is from thee gone, and thy
 body in earth raked,
Then thy body that was rank and undevout
 is all men's loathing maked.

Therefore, thou earth upon earth, that so
 wickedly hast wrought,
While that thou, earth, art upon earth, turn
 again thy thought;

And pray to that God upon earth that all
the earth hath wrought,
That thou, earth upon earth, unto bliss may
be brought.

O thou Lord, that madest this earth for this
earth, and suffered here sorrows ill,
Let never this earth for this earth his soul
spill;
But that this earth on this earth be ever
working thy will,
So that this earth from this earth may climb
up to thine high hill!

71. MAN'S CHOICE

Royal MS. Brit. Mus. (early XVth century)

HEAVEN is won with woe and shame,
Hell is won with glee and game.
I ask thee, therefore, of these two
On earth were better, weal or woe?

72. THE SINNER'S LAMENT

Harley MS. (end of XIVth century)

ALL the joy of our heart now is vanished
away;
Into sorrow and woe turned is all our
play.
The crown of our head is fallen to dust away;
That ever we sinned so sore, now we cry
" Welaway!"

73. A PRAYER AGAINST THE TIME OF OLD AGE

Lambeth MS. (c. 1430)

FROM the time that we were born
    Our youth passeth day by day,
  And age increaseth more and more,
And so doth it now, sooth to say.
Each hour life minisheth her store.
  So fast goeth our youth away,
And youth will come again no more,
  But age will make us bent and gray.
Therefore take heed both night and day
  How fast your youth doth time assuage,
And, young and old, let us all pray
  That God send us patience in our old age.

Our friends that should love us best
  Then will they have us but in hate;
In earthly friendship is no trust,
  And thereof are we aware too late.
Then may we sigh, " Ah, had I wist !"
  When our faint friends shall us forsake,
And then shall we go unkissed
  Both at the door and at the gate;
And for all the cheer that we can make,
  There is no joy in our visage,
When our beauty time shall slake,
  God send us patience in our old age.

All the life we lived here
   It is but as a dream met,
For now it is as it never were,
   And so is it that is coming yet.
Full fast we draw to our bier,
   In sorrow and dread should we be set;
The young then of the old may hear,
   But few thereby do benefit;
For the fiend hath caught them in his net,
   And holdeth them fast in bondage;
For they will not dispose their wit
   To have patience in their old age.

Then shall we see that worldly bliss
   Is but a thing of vanity,
And it maketh men to do amiss,
   That are in wealth and great beauty;
And therefore, Lord, right it is,
   With our own staff chastised to be;
Lord, give us grace to think of this,
   As thou boughtst us all upon a Tree;
And that we may in charity
   Well pass over our passage,
Into the bliss that aye shall be,
   God send us patience in our old age.

74. THE HEAVENLY JERUSALEM

" F. B. P." (*prob. Francis Baker, Priest and Recusant, c.* 1560)

JERUSALEM, my happy home,
    When shall I come to thee ?
  When shall my sorrows have an end,
    Thy joys when shall I see ?

O happy harbour of the saints !
    O sweet and pleasant soil !
In thee no sorrow may be found,
    No guilt, nor care, nor toil.

In thee no sickness may be seen,
    No hurt, nor ache, nor sore;
There is no death, nor ugly dole,
    But life for evermore.

No dampish mist is seen in thee,
    No cold nor darksome night;
There every soul shines as the sun;
    There God himself gives light.

There lust and lucre cannot dwell,
    There envy bears no sway;
There is no hunger, heat, nor cold,
    But pleasure every way.

Jerusalem, Jerusalem,
 God grant I once may see
Thine endless joys, and of the same
 Partaker aye to be !

Thy walks are made of precious stones,
 Thy bulwarks diamond square;
Thy gates are of right orient pearl
 Exceeding rich and rare.

Thy turrets and thy pinnacles
 With carbuncles do shine;
Thy very streets are paved with gold
 Surpassing clear and fine.

Thine houses are of ivory,
 Thy windows crystal clear;
Thy tiles are made of beaten gold,
 O God, that I were there !

Within thy gates doth nothing come,
 That is not passing clean,
No spider's web, no dirt, nor dust,
 Nor filth may there be seen.

Ah, my sweet home, Jerusalem,
 Would God I were in thee !
Would God my woes were at an end,
 Thy joys that I might see !

Our Lady sings Magnificat
 With tones surpassing sweet,
And all the virgins bear their part,
 Sitting about her feet.

Thy saints are crowned with glory great,
   They see God face to face;
They triumph still, they still rejoice;
   Most happy is their case.

We that are here in banishment
   Continually do moan:
We sigh and sob, we weep and wail,
   Perpetually we groan.

But there they live in such delight,
   Such pleasure and such play,
As that to them a thousand years
   Doth seem as yesterday.

Quite through the streets with silver sound
   The flood of life doth flow,
Upon whose banks on every side
   The wood of life doth grow.

There trees do evermore bear fruit,
   And evermore do spring;
There evermore the angels sit,
   And evermore do sing.

Jerusalem, my happy home,
   Would God I were in thee;
Would God my woes were at an end,
   Thy joys that I might see!

75. IN HEAVEN

Richard Rolle (c. 1340)

ALL manner of joys are in that stead;*
    There is life withouten death;
    And there is youth withouten eld;†
And there is all kind wealth to wield;
And there is rest without travail;
And there is all goods that never shall fail;
And there is peace withouten strife;
And there all manner of pleasant life;
And there is aye summer full bright to see,
And nevermore winter in that countrie;
And there is more worship and honour,
Than ever had king or emperor;
And there is melody of angel-song,
And there is praising them among;
And there is all friendship that may be,
And perfect love and charity.
And there is wisdom without folly,
And there is honesty without villainy.
All these a man may joys of heaven call;
But the most sovereign joy of all
Is sight of God's bright face,
In whom resteth all manner grace.

    * Place.   † Old age.